JOURNEY
THROUGH HELL

T0055263

JOURNEY THROUGH HELL

*Memoir of a World War II
American Navy Medic Captured
in the Philippines and Imprisoned
by the Japanese*

Loren E. Stamp

McFarland & Company, Inc., Publishers
Jefferson, North Carolina, and London

The present work is a reprint of the library bound edition of
Journey Through Hell: Memoir of a World War II American
Navy Medic Captured in the Philippines and Imprisoned
by the Japanese, *first published in 1993 by McFarland.*

Frontispiece: **The author, as a chief warrant officer, U.S. Navy, in 1955.**

LIBRARY OF CONGRESS CATALOGUING-IN-PUBLICATION DATA

Stamp, Loren E., 1919–
    Journey through hell : memoir of a World War II American
Navy medic captured in the Philippines and imprisoned by
the Japanese / Loren E. Stamp.
        p.   cm.
    Includes bibliographical references and index.

    ISBN 978-0-7864-6770-9
    softcover : acid free paper ∞

    1. World War, 1939–1945—Prisoners and prisons, Japanese.
    2. World War, 1939–1945—Personal narratives, American.
    3. Stamp, Loren E., 1919–   4. Prisoners of war—United
States—Biography.   5. Prisoners of war—Philippines—Biography.
    6. Surgeons—United States—Biography.   7. United States. Navy—
Biography.   8. World War, 1939–1945—Campaigns—Philippines—
Bataan (Province)   9. World War, 1939–1945—Philippines—
Corregidor Island.   I. Title.
    D805.J3S72 2012
    940.54'7252—dc20   92-51089

BRITISH LIBRARY CATALOGUING DATA ARE AVAILABLE

On the cover: *inset* surrender of U.S. forces on Corregidor Island at
the entrance to the Malinta Tunnel, May 1942 (United States Army
Center of Military History); aerial view of the ruins and a memorial
to American defenders of Corregidor Island during World War II
(photograph by David C. Maclean)

Manufactured in the United States of America

McFarland & Company, Inc., Publishers
  Box 611, Jefferson, North Carolina 28640
    www.mcfarlandpub.com

To my wife Helen,
our daughter Becky,
our son Larry
and our grandchildren

ACKNOWLEDGMENTS

The person to whom I am most grateful is my wife of 46 years, who helped nurture me back to health by understanding my needs and allowing me to recover in my own way. During the writing of this book, she has been especially helpful by allowing me the privacy that is needed to concentrate on writing. Without her this work would not have been possible.

Patty Caldwell spent many hours helping me with the word processor until I gained sufficient skill in its operation to accomplish what I set out to do. Not only that, she spent many hours editing and making suggestions to improve the presentation of my story. I am deeply indebted to her for any success which this story might have.

To everyone who helped in the preparation of this book, including Linda Kline and the staff at the TBE Office Equipment store who mimeographed untold numbers of copies while I waited, so I would not be delayed, my many thanks.

Very special thanks go to those who allowed me to use illustrations and excerpts from their publications: Dr. Paul Ashton; Dr. Eugene C. Jacobs, retired Army colonel; retired Army Lt. Gen. John M. Wright, Jr.; and Benjamin C. Steele, all former prisoners of war with whom I shared experiences. Each made major contributions to this book.

There were several others who made contributions to this effort, including Cdr. Robert E. Thompson, MSC, USN (Ret), and CDR Ernest J. Irvin, MSC, USN (Ret), both of whom were former shipmates and fellow POWs. Both of them read this script and offered editorial as well as historical comments. To these men I offer my most sincere thanks.

Loren E. Stamp
Summer 1993

CONTENTS

FOREWORD

This book, *Journey Through Hell*, is one man's experiences through World War II, with emphasis on the fighting on Bataan and Corregidor in the Philippine Islands and the subsequent journey through hell as a prisoner of war under the Japanese.

Loren Stamp and I first met as hospital corpsmen in 1940 at the U.S. Naval Hospital, Canacao, Philippine Islands. Navy policy required a year of duty ashore before we could be transferred to sea duty which everyone wanted. October 1940 found Stamp and me on the USS *Canopus*, a submarine tender, until his tour of duty ended and he was transferred ashore in early December 1941 to obtain transportation back to the United States. War intervened and delayed our return to the United States until September and October of 1945.

Since Navy medical department personnel are assigned to the Marine Corps, we both wound up with the 3rd Battalion, 4th Marine Regiment on Corregidor at Battery Point, after Bataan surrendered and we scuttled the USS *Canopus* to keep it from being captured by the Japanese. Stamp and I were carrying the dead on a litter one dark night after artillery from Bataan hit the search light.

After Corregidor surrendered, I was transferred to Bilibid in Manila and worked on the hospital staff for prisoners until December 13, 1944, when 1619 POWs were transferred to the *Oryoku Maru* for shipment to Japan. Stamp and I were united again and were together on the three different ships it took to get us to Japan. We were transferred to different POW camps in Kyushu, Japan, until the Japanese transferred the survivors to Korea and Mukden, Manchuria, where Stamp and I ended up.

I'm sure you will find the book informative, interesting, occasionally humorous, and sad, because of the loss of human life.

Other than Stamp, only one other hospital corpsman and I from the Medical-Dental Departments of the USS *Canopus* are alive today. All of the Navy doctors from the U.S. Naval Hospital Canacao are dead to the best of my knowledge.

In Their Memory I Remain,

Robert E. Thompson
CDR, MSC, USN (Ret)

INTRODUCTION

The year 1990 began with a beautiful, clear but cool, crisp day. It was a typically good Northwestern winter day, just the right kind of day to enjoy my usual early morning two-mile walk. Somehow, this day seemed to be something special. I had the feeling that this year might be different.

While I was on that walk, my thoughts went back to the night before, when I made my usual New Year's resolution. That resolution was to write about my experiences in Japanese prison camps during World War II. It was the same resolution I had made almost every year for many years. It was 45 years ago that I came home from a terrible experience, an experience that still haunts me at times. I needed to write about it.

Over the years, whenever conversation turned to my POW days, I would invariably be asked if I had written anything about those days. So many people have asked me about writing, and so many times I have tried, without success, that I began to feel guilty. For one thing, I have always thought that no one would believe some of the things that happened to me and to many others during those awful years. That made it difficult to start writing. This day, however, I was determined to sit down and start as soon as I returned home. I made a vow that day to stop procrastinating and start producing.

I think I can attribute this resolve, for the most part to our son Larry and daughter Becky. Becky has been especially pesky, and seems to have developed a newfound interest in the stories that I have told over the years. Larry has frequently reminded me of the promises I have made in the past. I dedicate this effort to both of them, and to their mother, my wife Helen, who has done so much to help me through the recovery years.

At the outset, I should caution the reader to be aware that, while I can recall vividly nearly every experience during those POW years, it is very difficult to remember dates since I had no calendar and kept no records. For practical purposes, I have taken the liberty of using dates from the available official records and the many books about the subject. All of the Japanese POWs went through a similar hell, but each of us experienced it differently. What I hope to do is relate my own experiences as much as possible. It is not my intention to compete with others relating their stories, but to write my memoirs for my family and friends.

Some of the men kept diaries, which they were able to hide through the terrible times. I never thought to keep a diary. My main concern, during those years, was just to stay alive and I only did what I had to do to accomplish this. While I fended for myself, I never knowingly did anything to survive at the expense of another person, unless that person happened to be a Japanese guard. I can't deny that.

The Veterans Administration has labeled me a "survivor." I'm not sure of their definition of the word, but everyone knows that survival is a natural instinct in all living things. I believe that, in addition to instinct, survival depends a lot on knowledge of survival techniques, which all of us have either been taught, or learned from experience. To natural instinct, and learning through experience, I would add *luck*. While I had the natural instinct, and some experience in survival, most of the life-threatening situations I found myself in were new and unusual, as well as unexpected. I think sometimes my survival depended on being in the right place at the right time. I hope, through this book, to make people aware of my plight, as well as the plight of many others, in the service of our country during World War II.

"I am Laertes' son, Odysseus. Men hold me formidable for guile in peace and war...."
    —Homer, Book IX, *The Odyssey* (circa 800 B.C.)

"It was the best of times, it was the worst of times, it was the age of wisdom, it was the age of foolishness...."
    —Charles Dickens, Chapter I, *A Tale of Two Cities* (1859)

"Many of the children had been permitted to sit up beyond their usual bedtime. A small band of them were lying on their stomachs on the floor looking at the colored sheets of the comic papers...."
    —Kate Chopin, Chapter IX, *The Awakening* (1899)

"...the stuff dreams are made of...."
    —Humphrey Bogart as Sam Spade in *The Maltese Falcon* (1941)

"I wonder how Dick Tracy made out today."
    —Elmer Fudd, "Elmer's Pet Rabbit" (1941)

"When you combine realism and the fantastic, you've got a story every time."
    —Chester Gould, *Editor and Publisher* (1956)

CHAPTER 1

One of my earliest memories as a child was watching the parades that would be held on Memorial Day and Armistice Day. The time was shortly after World War I, and I was fascinated by soldiers and sailors in uniform. Wanting to be a soldier, in those days, was typical of 4- and 5-year-olds. I was always playing soldier around the house, with my newspaper fore-and-aft hat and wooden sword.

On one occasion, after the parade, my Dad talked to me about soldiers and sailors, and a little bit about war. He told me that, when I grew up, if I had to go into the service, I should join the Navy because sailors live on clean ships, while soldiers fight wars in the mud trenches and had "all kinds of bugs."

When I grew up, I remembered his advice. While I had not intended to go into the service, it was the middle of the Great Depression, and there was no work. Shortly after I finished high school, I took the Navy physical, and waited to be called. In those days it was not easy to get into the Navy. No one could get in without a high school diploma, and there was a long waiting list.

Uncle John (Mother's brother) managed to get me into the Civilian Conservation Corps. I was eligible because I had no home or income, so I took advantage of the program. At least I would have board and room.

The CCC was managed by the Army, and the men wore Army uniforms, leggings, and the whole works. We even did close-order drill. Our pay was $35 a month, and we were allowed to keep $5. The rest went to our families. In my case, my sister Toni was the beneficiary. She would keep it for me.

After about four months in the CCC, the Navy notified me that if I could still pass the physical, I could get in the Navy. This was just after Christmas of 1934.

My status in the CCC at the time the Navy called me was precarious at best, and I was worried about being accepted by the Navy. I had gone to Detroit over the Thanksgiving holiday, and failed to return on time because I was hospitalized with pneumonia. For that offense, I was fined $1 for every day I was AWOL, a period of nine days. I was afraid that this might go on my record preventing my entry into the Navy. After a talk with the camp commander, I was advised that if I wanted to go to Detroit, I could be discharged from the CCC but I would not be eligible for leave. That meant that if I were not accepted by the Navy, I could not come back to camp.

On January 7, I left the camp in Northern Michigan, at 0300 (3 AM), and walked about four miles to the train. The temperature was 35 degrees below zero. In Detroit I signed up for the Navy on January 9, 1935, and left immediately for the Naval Training Center, Norfolk, Virginia, for recruit training.

When I reported in at the Naval Training Center, I was still wearing the Army uniform from the CCC. I felt foolish because this attracted more than a little attention. The company commander knew that I could march in close-order formation. This meant that he thought I could help others. At first I was assigned as a squad leader for the hours of marching. I continued this duty until someone discovered that I had brought my trumpet with me (I had played the bugle in CCC camp).

When the shuffling was through, I was assigned to the station band for drills, and to the officer's swimming pool for lifeguard duty, when not drilling. On Saturday nights I played in the station orchestra, which played for dances and special events. I was having a ball.

Following training I was assigned to the seagoing unit, while waiting orders for sea duty. In the seagoing unit we mustered every morning, and heard the list of transfers read. I hoped to be assigned soon because the chief petty officer of the unit was a tyrant. If he saw a dirty seabag, he would make the culprit crawl under the barracks, dragging his seabag on the ground behind him. After that, he made the culprit scrub his seabag and wash all the clothes in it. Somehow I lucked out.

About two weeks later, at muster, there was a change in routine.

Instead of reading the names of the transferees, the chief called our attention to the USS *Missouri* (the original one), docked at the main pier. We could all see the huge battleship, and I wondered what was coming. I didn't trust the chief. He called for volunteers from the men who played instruments in the station band or orchestra, and would like to serve aboard that ship. He said that several members of the ship's band were leaving because of expired enlistments, and the ship was looking for replacements. To make it more attractive, he added that the *Missouri* was making a midshipmen's cruise to Europe the following month. That got my attention. When four of us volunteered, he told us to get our seabags, and climb into the pickup nearby.

All four of us climbed into the back of the pickup, sat down, and after our orders were handed to the driver, we took off down the street toward the *Missouri*. I was dreaming about what it would be like, when the truck made a sharp left turn and headed for the main gate. We all pounded on the cab of the truck. Finally the truck stopped. The driver got out and told us that our orders read that we were to be transferred to the Hospital Corps School in Portsmouth, across the bay from Norfolk.

I was stunned and I knew that the others were too. There was really nothing we could do. So, we reported to the commanding officer of the Naval Hospital for duty. He met us in person, probably aware that this kind of hijacking had gone on before. In a fatherly way he asked us if we had thought about whether all we had to do was play music. He asked us if we were aware that we would have to scrub decks and chip paint, like all the others. Then he advised us that we should try the Hospital Corps School. If we didn't like it we could always go to sea.

We all tried it. We all served more than twenty years in that Corps, either enlisted or commissioned. Thus began my 56-year career in the health care field. While I was angry at the time, the new challenge consumed me, and it became the best thing that could have happened to me. After retirement from the Navy in 1959 I earned degrees in nursing and public health from California State University, Chico, California. I never again, though, played the trumpet.

Following graduation from the Hospital Corps School in August 1935 I was transferred to the U.S. Naval Hospital, Newport, Rhode Island, where I spent the remaining three and a half years of my first enlistment.

Three things stand out in my memory of those years in Newport. One was the rugged work schedule. Second was the knowledge and skills I gained in the nursing field. The third was the friendliness of the New England people.

3

I referred to the work schedule as rugged. At first it was formidable. The "work" schedule was really two schedules: one was the regular work schedule, and the other was the duty (watch) schedule. The work schedule was related to one's regular work assignment (usually a hospital ward with 25-30 patients), while the duty schedule referred to one's assignment to "watch" status, which referred to the time one had to be available any time and any place needed.

Work schedules were so arranged much like they are in civilian life. Duty schedules were arranged on a 24-hour basis, that is, 24 hours on and 24 hours off, known in the Navy as the Port and Starboard Watch Schedule. That meant that 50 percent of the staff was always on duty in any 24-hour period. Those on duty would work on the wards from 0700 (7 AM) until 2100 (9 PM), and then work three or four hours on special duty (usually caring for a critically ill patient needing special care during the night), for a total of 18 hours or more of work on their duty day. On their off-duty day, they would work from 0700 to 1630 (4:30 PM). By doubling up on the duty schedule for the weekends, 50 percent of the staff could have liberty from 1630 Friday to 0700 Monday, while the other 50 percent of the staff would work through the weekend, followed by a nine-hour work day, or a possible 63 hours of work in a period of 81 hours. I considered that a rugged schedule.

It took several months for me to become acclimated to the Port and Starboard schedule. During that time, liberty, for me, was a time for rest because of fatigue. As time went on, I learned how to adjust to the schedule, and even trade a watch occasionally, to get an extra day off.

My enlistment expired on January 8, 1939, and I couldn't wait to get out of the Navy. I had no love for the Navy, and I felt lucky that I hadn't been court-martialed. I was close a few times, but I was lucky.

I had made tentative plans to try medical school. I had arranged to live with a family in Richmond, Virginia, who were relatives of a patient I had cared for. I was to work in their business while attending the University of Richmond.

I was paid off on January 8, 1939, and hitchhiked to New York City, where I stayed in the YMCA for a few days. I then continued on to Richmond, and contacted the family with whom I would be living. Within two weeks I had been denied admission, and gave up plans to go to college.

My next move was to return to Detroit and stay with Uncle Charlie (Dad's brother), while I looked for work. It was now the last week in January 1939, and the country was still in the grips of the Great

Depression. For the next two months, I continued to look for work and found nothing.

It was mid–March, and my chances of finding work before the first of April were dwindling. If I did have to go back into the Navy, I would have to reenlist before April 9th or lose my rating. The only alternative I had was to go to work for the federal government at the leper colony in Carville, Louisiana. That job called for a ten-year commitment, at $10,000 per year with all expenses paid—a fortune in those days.

In addition to the problem of finding work, there was the political instability in Europe, with war imminent. The more I thought about my predicament, the more my rational self told me that the service probably wasn't the worst place to be. In either event, I would have a place to sleep and food to eat. Of the two alternatives, the service seemed the best.

CHAPTER 2

On April 7, 1939, I went to the recruiting office in Detroit, and agreed to re-enlist if I could go to China for duty. My rationale was to avoid the war in Europe. I felt that my decision was reasonable. Time would tell. On that same day, I was on a train bound for San Francisco, for further transfer to the Asiatic-Pacific area for duty.

On arrival in San Francisco, I reported immediately to the Naval Station, Yurba Buena Island. I was informed that I was scheduled to leave in about ten days, aboard the Navy transport USS *Chaumont*. In the interim, I was assigned to various work details, including military escort for funerals of war veterans.

A few days later, I fractured a bone in my foot, and was transferred to the Naval Hospital at Mare Island. This caused a change, delaying my orders overseas. I was transferred back to Treasure Island about the first of May, with orders to proceed to the Orient aboard the first available Navy transport, which happened to be the USS *Henderson*, sailing on May 29, 1939.

On May 9, a friend and I went to San Francisco on liberty. I had sold all my civilian clothes, so I had to wear my uniform, and my friend wore his. We had made an agreement that there would be no girls. We would just take in a show, have dinner and return to the base. I don't remember the name of the show, but I do remember remarking to my friend about the beautiful redhead in the chorus line on stage after the film. He nodded in agreement, and that was that.

After the show, we walked down Market Street, taking in the sights and sounds of one of the most interesting streets in the world. I'll never forget the music on nearly every jukebox in almost every storefront, the "Beer Barrel Polka."

Eventually, we found a good restaurant and entered. We ordered drinks, and studied the menu to find something we could afford. Before the waiter returned to take our order, another waiter approached our table and asked if we knew when the *Henderson* was leaving. When I asked who wanted to know, he pointed to a young lady a few tables away. I couldn't believe my eyes. There was the same young lady we had seen on the stage earlier.

I told the waiter to tell the girl that we would answer her question if she would have a drink with us. A few minutes later she came over to our table and sat down. We ordered a drink for her and started to talk. My friend reminded me that we had agreed there would be no girls, and he got up and left.

Ten days later, that girl, Roberta Ann "Bobbie" Robertson and I were married at City Hall in San Francisco. On May 29, I said goodbye to Bobbie and boarded the *Henderson* for the Far East. Little did I know that I would never see her again.

The trip was boring, except for stops in Hawaii and Guam. I spent some of my time on KP (kitchen police), and the rest of my time, during the day, waiting in line for chow. The chow lines were so long that most of us would get up earlier than usual just to get in line for breakfast, eat, wash our utensils, and get in line again for lunch. After lunch, we would repeat the procedure for dinner. After dinner, we would sleep until morning. Any spare time we had was usually spent playing pinochle, acey-deucy, and sometimes poker, when we could find an out-of-the-way place.

Seventeen days later, we arrived at the Cavite Navy Yard, Philippine Islands. I had been notified en route that my duty station would be the Naval Hospital at Canacao, just across a small bay from Cavite. It was then that I found out that our tour of duty in the Orient consisted of 15 months ashore at Canacao, followed by 12 months at sea.

I had made up my mind, after talking to many men who had had duty in the tropics, to avoid some of the problems they had experienced. I knew that 10 percent of those who had served in the Philippines were sent home with a diagnosis of mental illness. I didn't intend to return that way. To avoid the usual social problems, I took up tennis and bowling and I played center field for the hospital's softball team.

7

U.S. Naval Hospital, Canacao, P.I. prior to World War II (photo courtesy Department of the Navy, Bureau of Medicine and Surgery).

I was lucky enough to buy a small 14-foot sailboat from a man who was returning to the States. That boat gave me many hours of pleasure, although I never learned the art of sailing. One other man at the hospital liked to sail, so we always went together. We always stayed inside the small bay, which was fairly protected. The area was the landing and take-off path for the China clipper flying boats, which came in once a week. Many times the boat would capsize on us, and the Navy Yard would send one of their "680" boats to pick us up and tow the boat back to Canacao.

In July of 1940, I was transferred to the USS *Canopus,* a submarine tender with the Asiatic Fleet in Manila, about 30 miles across Manila Bay. While we were in port, I bought some clubs and took up golf. Then a good friend talked me into joining the boxing team, which I did mostly for the physical conditioning. The coach was a former all–Navy lightweight champion and was the boxing coach at the Naval Academy for several years. I was in great physical shape at 165 pounds.

Three times a week, early in the morning, I would go ashore with the boxing team for a five-mile run around the Walled City Intramuros, an old Spanish fort in Manila. Workouts were aboard ship in the evenings, which made for a full day. I fought in several "smokers" during

8

the next year and never won a single fight, but I was fast and never got hurt.

Beginning in the fall of 1940, the fleet made a number of RWT (Readiness for War Trial) runs, in preparation for possible war. In addition, we spent much of our time in the southern islands trying to hide from the Japanese Navy which we knew was on the prowl.

It was during one of those RWT runs on the *Sealion* that I had an unexpected brush with death. The *Sealion* was attacking a target ship. We were about 400 feet below the surface, in 35,000 feet of water. We fired a torpedo (not live), and nobody could track it toward its target. After several minutes, the skipper ordered us to surface, and we returned to the *Canopus*. When the stern was raised out of the water, there was the torpedo. It had turned about an inch after it had left the tube. When the air pressure failed, the torpedo came back into the tube. If the torpedo had not turned about an inch before it came back into the tube, we would have sank in 35,000 feet of water. My life had come within an inch of being over. I would have missed the war.

During the last six months of 1941, while still attached to the submarine tender USS *Canopus*, I was assigned TAD (temporary additional duty), at different times, to three of the new SEA class boats, tended by the *Canopus*. These boats were the latest in underwater technology. Those TAD assignments were to relieve the regularly assigned hospital corpsman, usually due to illness, leave or unexpected transfer. At that time I was not qualified by rate for independent submarine duty, but was considered for the task when I volunteered.

The boats that I served on were the USS *Shark*, USS *Porpoise* and the USS *Sealion*. I was on the *Sealion* when I received orders to return to the States. I had already been held past my regular tour of duty, which would have ended in October of 1941, but because of a shortage of qualified hospital corpsmen, some of us were asked to stay a little longer. I was elated to be going home at last to be with my wife.

On December 7, 1941, I was transferred to the Naval Hospital at Canacao, Sangley Point, Philippines, for further transfer to the States via the President Line's, SS *Coolidge*. Several of us were returning at the same time, so our orders were to escort a group of mental patients back to the States.

At the time of my transfer off the *Sealion*, the boat was under major engine overhaul at the Cavite Navy Yard, not too far from the hospital. Most of the crew was living ashore while the boat was being repaired. This was to be significant the following day. Early the next morning, I was asleep in the barracks at the hospital when I was awakened by Chris, the houseboy. Chris was going quietly from bed to bed, telling

those just awakened that the radio was reporting that America was at war; Pearl Harbor had been bombed by the Japanese. (December 7th in Hawaii was December 8th in the Philippines due to the International Dateline.) As I rolled out of bed, I was aware that nearly everyone else was already up. The conversation, as one might expect, was focused on the Japanese attack on Pearl Harbor.

The general consensus was not so much surprise at the attack, but it was our view that the Japs were really stupid to attack Hawaii. Didn't they know how strong our Navy was? It was generally agreed that the Japs (we no longer called them Japanese) had really sealed their fate when they attacked America. The war wouldn't last long. From the conversation, I noted a general feeling that everything would be over in short order. No one seemed to think that we would even get involved here in the Philippines.

Those who were on duty reported to their assigned stations. Those of us being transferred packed our seabags and prepared to leave. Meanwhile, those not on duty could not sleep, so the talk continued. Several times I heard the words "It will be over in a week." "Frisco brew in 42" was the cry. Most agreed that it couldn't possibly last a month. As the morning wore on, I continued preparation for leaving by early afternoon to board the SS *Coolidge* for home.

My orders were cancelled. Tuesday was a continuation of Monday. Talk continued about the war, as we began to hear reports of bombing at Clark Field and Japanese planes over Manila.

On Wednesday, at lunchtime, I wandered over to the mess hall. While I was eating, I began to hear what sounded like the Cavite Navy Yard's noon whistle. Then I suddenly realized that it wasn't noon, and the whistle wasn't stopping. Before long I realized that the sound might indeed be an air raid. The anxiety around the tables was obvious, and in the absence of specific instructions, most of us left our lunch and headed for the Master-at-Arms office. Before we could get there someone yelled from the mess hall doorway, "AIR RAID—ALL HANDS TAKE COVER." A chill descended on the mess hall.

Opposite: **The USS *Canopus*, submarine tender, part of the Asiatic Fleet, tied up in Manila Bay, 1941. The boats tied up alongside are World War I submarines (photo courtesy National Archives).**

CHAPTER 3

For the first time there was a feeling of apprehension. As I headed outdoors to crawl under the wooden hospital building for protection, I felt real terror for the first time. I couldn't see anything, and heard very little. After a period of suspense, I could hear the rumble of planes overhead and some explosions coming from the direction of the Navy Yard. It was scary to look out and see the bombers directly overhead. It was then that I knew the war was really on.

After what seemed like forever, a truck pulled alongside the hospital building and the driver called to us to get aboard. Quickly, we boarded the flat-bed truck, and raced out of the hospital gate toward the Navy Yard.

We had each been given a medical aid kit before we left. I was glad at least to have something to do. The suspense was terrible. If I had been alone I don't think that I could have functioned, but in the company of people who were sharing the same experience, I was able to keep my fear under control.

From a distance we could see smoke and flames, and as we got closer to the main gate we could not believe the carnage. The Navy Yard was devastated. There wasn't a building left standing. The devastation extended for some distance outside the Navy Yard perimeter fence, into the shacks of the surrounding community. I didn't have time to sightsee. I knew what I was there for, and it didn't take long for me to get to work.

As we left the truck, there was a distinct odor of newly mown grass. I didn't recognize it, but someone yelled, "poison gas," and then I remembered that phosgene, an extremely toxic gas, smelled like newly mown grass. For a minute there was indecision. Then we realized that if it had been phosgene, we would all have been dead. The point was moot anyway, for we had no gas masks. At the first stop, just outside the Navy Yard gate, there were many dead and wounded. It was obvious that someone had already been there ahead of us because a few had bandages.

All were Filipino workers who had gone outside the main gate to eat their lunches, and had been sitting next to shacks which lined the street, as was the custom. They didn't have a chance. After checking several bodies along the roadside, I came upon a Filipino with his huge straw hat down over his eyes, as if at siesta. He was sitting against one of the buildings. My first impression was that he was just waiting there, asleep. I reached over to grab his arm to help him up, and as I did, his head just rolled down onto his lap. I was momentarily stunned.

We made our way into the Navy Yard, looking through the rubble. We found scores of dead but few wounded. Some of the less seriously wounded were helping to move others, more seriously wounded, toward the dock area for evacuation to the hospital which was about a mile across the bay.

I approached one of the piers and saw a large number of wounded who had been arranged in groups according to the severity of their condition. The most critically wounded were being loaded onto one of the Torpedo Squadron boats and taken to the hospital. This would continue on into the evening until all of the Americans had been evacuated. The sorting of wounded continued, and we were kept busy repositioning them for more comfort, or giving morphine to those in greatest pain.

One of the Americans, obviously a civilian, was lying on his back under a blanket near the pier. At first glance I did not see any evidence of a wound, but he was obviously in great pain, and in some shock. Noting the tag on his shirt, I knew that he had been given morphine, so I proceeded on to other wounded. Shortly after this I was called back to the pier area to help load the wounded onto the available PT boat. When I got to the civilian I had just checked, four of us lifted the man onto a litter for transport. I noticed that as we placed him on the litter his legs hung strangely off the end of the litter in such a way that his problem became obvious—both legs had been neatly severed about halfway between the ankle and the knee, with only some skin on the back of his legs keeping them from being completely detached. Because it was very difficult to put him on the PT boat due to his dangling legs, I reached into my medical kit, took out my bandage shears and cut the remaining skin to release both lower legs, and placed them both on the stretcher with him. I don't know what happened to him. The last I saw of him he was on his way to surgery.

After the evacuation of wounded from the Navy Yard, all those in the detail I was with were assigned patient care. Many of those wounded died during the evening and night hours. At one time, during the evening, the trucks carrying the bodies from the hospital to the temporary morgue area could not keep up with work load, so bodies were stored in every available space. I have no idea how many casualties there were, but the number must have been in the hundreds.

I later learned that for his extraordinary work during the enemy raid on the Navy Yard, and later for his efforts in evacuating casualties, the commander of the PT (Patrol Torpedo) Boat Squadron was awarded the Congressional Medal of Honor. He deserved it.

On Tuesday the hospital was ordered to evacuate all patients who could be moved, as well as the staff. Those patients who could not be routinely relocated were later taken by buses to Army Sternberg Hospital at Fort McKinley in Manila. The day was hectic to say the least. All moving vehicles capable of carrying personnel were commandeered for the task. In addition to land vehicles, all Navy craft were put to use to move hospital patients and medical personnel across the bay to Manila where they were picked up and transported to a small Catholic college campus, Santa Scholastica, on the outskirts of Manila.

The next few days were spent building up a field hospital in preparation for assignment wherever needed. We had no uniforms, except our whites, so we dipped our whites in strong coffee. The effect was not bad. "Mustard colored commandos" was our nickname.

Several of the hospital corpsmen were assigned to outlying naval units, as well as to the Army Sternberg Hospital at Fort McKinley. A close buddy of mine and I were assigned to the 4th Marine Corps Regiment to set up a field hospital in Bataan. On the night before our departure I was handed the keys to a large truck carrying the equipment. My truck would head a convoy. The battalion medical officer was a Navy commander, and would ride with me. I sure wasn't looking forward to the run of about 100 miles of main highway, much of it without cover. My friend was to ride the back of the truck to warn of enemy aircraft. With the truck keys in my pocket, my friend and I talked about the next day, and what we were about to get into. Both of us knew a little about

14

the Marines, and the little that we knew made us apprehensive. We knew that the Marines were always on the front lines, and that scared the hell out of us. Thoughts of the front lines did not fit in with why I joined the Navy.

We stewed over our predicament, and both came to the conclusion that our free time was limited, so we decided to head for Manila to see a couple of girls we knew while we had the chance. Since there were no guards and no gates, we took off and headed the 15 miles to Manila. Getting to Manila was no problem. There was considerable traffic so we were able to hitchhike rides. Our convoy was to leave at 0600 (6 AM) and we knew we had to be back no later than 0500 (5 AM) so we started back about 0300 (3 AM). We hadn't considered the lack of traffic, however. We should have known that there would be fewer vehicles in the middle of the night than when we went into Manila. There was no public transportation.

We were feeling confident that we would be back in plenty of time, but when an hour had passed and we still had no ride, we started to get concerned. We had about 15 miles to travel and there was no way that we could make it back on foot. As time went by we began to panic.

We continued to walk and the realization that we were AWOL began to sink in. We sweated over our AWOL situation, and started to wonder: What if we were declared deserters? Knowing the penalty for desertion in wartime was the firing squad, there was no doubt in either of our minds that we were in deep trouble. I had a knot in the pit of my stomach. The war was only a few hours old and I was about to get shot for desertion.

Nearly two hours had passed and those two hours seemed like an eternity. My friend finally spotted a delivery truck. We waved frantically and the driver came to a stop. At first he refused to help us, but a 20-peso bill caught his attention, and we climbed aboard. In a short time we arrived at the college campus. It was 0530 (5:30 AM) when he left us near a wooded area. We proceeded through the woods until we reached the staging area, which was some distance from the Command Center. As I mentioned before, there were no gates and no guards. Still we were not over our panic. We had not yet met anyone, and we began to think of what we would say when we did.

We arrived at the staging area (where vehicles, equipment and troups assemble for movement) and tried to blend in with the rest of the men assigned to the convoy. We milled around the men who were checking the vehicles and the loads ready for take-off, when Commander Hayes spotted us and yelled, "Where in the hell have you guys been? We've been looking for you for an hour." Before either of us could answer, Commander Hayes said to me, "Stamp, do you have the keys to the lead truck?" I replied, "Yes, sir!"

Our anxiety only increased as we busied ourselves with things that needed to be done. As the time to leave approached and still there was no indication that we had been missed during the night, I put the keys in the ignition of the truck and prepared to leave on command.

What we did not know at the time was that a number of the other men on the detail had slept in the woods the previous night. This might explain why we were not questioned further about our disappearance. When we were ready to go, I felt considerably better, but not completely at ease. The next few hours were busy and the episode of the previous night began to fade. I was now beginning to feel that the episode of the night before was forgotten.

The road to Bataan was wide open with few places to pull off in case of strafing, and we could see Jap fighters over Manila Bay. It was imperative that everybody keep a sharp lookout for planes in our area. As it turned out, we stopped only twice to pull off the road into the rice paddies until the air was clear of enemy planes. I felt much better when we reached the safety of the jungle, which covered much of the road to Mariveles, our destination. The trip was otherwise uneventful.

When we reached Mariveles, we were directed to the area where we were to set up our batallion hospital. This task took us until well into the next day. When that was finished I was directed to take the truck and proceed to Olongapo about 100 miles to the north. Olongapo had been a small ship repair facility, with a dry dock capable of handling submarines and some smaller ships. There was a Navy dispensary there, and security was handled by a Marine unit. It was this unit and their light equipment that I was sent to evacuate back to Bataan. I was issued a .45 caliber pistol, and an armed guard was assigned to accompany me. Except for the gun on my belt, I was getting used to war—and it was indeed war!

The outgoing trip was a nightmare. Thousands of Filipinos were retreating back into Bataan. There were no vehicles so they plodded their way on foot. The night was black and quiet, and it was difficult to see the Filipinos. On several occasions, the walking troops stepped in front of the truck to stop it and then attempted to make me turn around, wanting me to drive them to Bataan. I was glad to see daylight, even though enemy planes would make it more dangerous.

At Olongapo we loaded men and equipment as quickly as possible, and found that we still had room in the truck, so we loaded some freshly baked bread from the Chinese bakery on the base, and headed back to Bataan. The return trip was uneventful.

CHAPTER 4

When I got back to Battalion Headquarters, I was told to report to the Company Headquarters of a Marine unit that was being sent to Corregidor for beach defense, since there was no infantry to defend the "Rock."

The Rock was an island fortress located in the mouth of Manila Bay in the Philippines. It was the largest of four such islands. It was defended by several batteries of coast artillery heavy guns, including 12-inch, 14-inch and 16-inch cannons, 12-inch mortars, all in fixed positions facing seaward. The only mobile artillery pieces were 155mm howitzers. There was *no* infantry on the Rock.

Since all of the large guns on Corregidor were aimed toward the sea to protect the mouth of Manila Bay, the Japs ignored Corregidor and concentrated on landing troops both north and south of Manila Bay. Initial Jap landings at Linguyan Gulf in the north were so successful that the Americans were caught by surprise and had to retreat back toward Bataan. This partially explained why I had so much trouble on the trip to Olongapo.

On Corregidor I was assigned to Company C of the 3rd Battalion of the 4th Marine Regiment. We arrived on the Rock a few days before Christmas 1941. Corregidor had not seen any of the war at this point. Things seemed to be business as usual, except for total blackouts at night to make it difficult for enemy bombers to see the big gun emplacements. We spent the next few days getting organized and preparing to assume our positions at various beach locations.

During the first few days we were billeted in Middleside Barracks which was located halfway between Bottomside Dock Area and Topside, which was the highest elevation on the Rock. The power plant and the cold storage plant were located at Bottomside, about halfway along the length of the narrow island and there were dock facilities on both sides of the island. "Officer's Country" was located Topside, with the old hospital located in the same general area.

On the opposite end of the Rock, several hundred yards from the dock area, there was a hill several hundred feet high, which had been tunneled through with a main tunnel and several laterals, many with cross connections. This was caled Malinta Tunnel and it contained Command Control, a huge hospital, complete with surgical, medical and diagnostic facilities. Also stored in Malinta Tunnel was a considerable supply of canned and packaged provisions and large caches of ammunition, consisting mostly of shells for the coastal guns, as well as small arms and ammunition.

Prior to World War II, the concept of war was predicated on the belief that if one side could capture the other side's capital, the whole country would capitulate. The entire Rock had been fortified so that it could withstand attacks from the sea, in the event the enemy would try to attack Manila, the capital. The only problem was that no one told the Japanese. From the very beginning their strategy was to bypass the island fortresses (there were three smaller islands similarly fortified) and attack Manila only after all defensive units were backed up into Bataan, then arrange to clear the harbor by attacking the fortresses from shore-based artillery located on both sides of the entry to the harbor. That is why the Japs had to take the Bataan Peninsula before they could concentrate their efforts on Corregidor and the other islands.

The prevailing feeling on Christmas Eve 1941 was that the Japs would be stupid to attack the Rock. We had no idea of the devastation at Pearl Harbor, and I think that some of us felt that the quiet meant that American troops and fleet were giving the Japs hell elsewhere. Morale was high.

Some time around noon, the air raid siren sounded. Those who had been on Corregidor since the beginning went about their usual routine, while those of us who had just arrived headed for cover. Most of my detachment had seen the awful carnage at Cavite, and we were not taking chances.

At the time of the siren my group was billeted in one end of Middleside Barracks, popularly known as Mile Long Barracks. It consisted of three stories of reinforced concrete and steel.

By the time that everyone else discovered that this was a real air raid, my unit was packed on the deck space on the ground floor of Middleside Barracks. I was one of the first to get under cover and was nearly crushed by the weight of those who came in late.

Just as the space was filling up, there was a tremendous explosion and we were covered with dust and debris. I was so packed underneath the mass that I could hardly see. A short time later, there were calls for help from the outside. As we scrambled to get untangled and get out we noticed that three of the four walls were leaning precariously inward, threatening to collapse. We had received a direct hit just above us on the top floor. My ears were still ringing from the terrible noise of the explosion.

Outside the building there was chaos. Wounded and dead were strewn everywhere and the cries of the wounded drowned out even the noise of the planes overhead. We immediately went to work helping those that we could, and trying to put them under cover. All the while Japanese fighter planes were shooting at anything that moved. Japanese bombers overhead made unimpeded runs the entire length of the Rock.

Someone had commandeered a large truck and we proceeded to load as many as we could of the most seriously wounded. A call came for volunteers to go with the truck taking the wounded to the hospital in Malinta Tunnel, and I was one of several volunteers. As we proceeded down the treacherous road to Bottomside, we were strafed several times but escaped injury. It was like a nightmare.

We unloaded and started back to our positions to bring more wounded to the hospital. We were halfway back when the all clear siren sounded. The remainder of the day was spent taking several loads of wounded to the hospital, while Army burial details picked up the dead. Fortunately the number of casualties was small considering the other damage that was done. Needless to say, everyone was more prepared for the almost continuous bombing during the following weeks.

As soon as we had secured our area, my Marine unit was deployed to a beach defense area on the Bataan side of the Rock. This location included a large pill box command post directly on the beach with machine gun emplacements located appropriately. About 30 feet above the beach, looking toward the summit of the Rock, there was a large searchlight mounted on tracks and concealed in a tunnel for protection when not in use. This light would be brought out at night and turned on to scan the water toward Bataan. Then it was quickly returned to its protective tunnel. The mouth of the tunnel was at a right angle to the

20

beach line and to the coast of Bataan Peninsula. This procedure was supposed to prevent the enemy from zeroing in on the light with their artillery.

A few yards further up the incline was a large tunnel with an entrance at a right angle to the beach line, like the search light tunnel, for protection from enemy fire. This was used primarily for storage of artillery shells for the large guns located further up the Rock. The position was called Battery Point, probably because of its location on a small promontory, and because of the big gun battery located above our beach position.

The tunnel was the obvious location for our aid station, because it was centrally located among the troop positions and because of its protection. For the next day or two, we busied ourselves with learning the positions of the Marines so that we would know where to go to provide medical help for injuries caused by the bombing and shelling in our area.

Our medical officer was a Navy lieutenant commander named Hogshire, who turned out to be an excellent doctor as well as a good leader.

Also with our aid station was a Navy lieutenant doctor, a Navy lieutenant dentist, and four or five hospital corpsmen, one of whom I remember was Robert E. Thompson (from the *Canopus*). The corpsmen were usually assigned to the platoon positions in the field, with one or two usually assigned to the aid station. During the months of January, February, and part of March the bombings continued with monotonous regularity. It seemed like the air raid siren was screaming continuously. At one time we had an arrangement where one or two persons would spot the planes and watch for the bombs to be released. The rest of us would continue whatever we were doing. At the signal "bombs away," everybody would hit their foxholes or other cover, and stay down until the bombs hit. Then we would continue on, providing our area didn't get hit.

During this time there were infrequent night bombings using phosphorous, which sticks to anything it touches and burns on contact. These bombs were nuisances more than threats, because we were

Opposite, top: **Ground view of "Mile Long Barracks." This photo was taken in 1987 and does not show the damage done by the Japanese December 1941 to May 1942.** *Bottom:* **Aerial view of "Mile Long Barracks." This 1987 photo shows about one-third of the barracks destroyed by the Japanese. I was on the ground floor of the destroyed portion during the first Japanese air raid on Christmas Day, 1941 (photos courtesy Asbury L. Nix, former POW).**

21

always fighting fires at night and dodging bombs during the day. We lived, slept and ate in foxholes or tunnels.

Meanwhile the battle for the Philippines was reaching fever pitch as American and Filipino forces had retreated back to Bataan and a large Japanese land force was pushing them farther and farther back toward Mariveles. In addition to the military, thousands and thousands of Filipino civilians had backed up into Bataan, creating severe problems with supplies, especially food. There was an adequate supply of weapons for a long battle and enough food for the military for a short battle, but not enough food for the estimated 30,000 civilians. Some of the soldiers, who later escaped to Corregidor, reported that in the latter part of March, rations were down to one can of salmon for four men per day. There was no chance of continuing without starvation, so on April 9 (my birthday), troops in Bataan were ordered to surrender.

Despite tremendous logistic problems, the American and Filipino troops had endured well until the food supply diminished. The American and Filipino soldiers (known as FilAmericans), about 50,000 strong, held off a well trained Japanese Army of over 200,000 men for nearly four months.

While morale remained fair on the Rock, the fall of Bataan affected us seriously. Where was the help we were supposed to be getting? Where were the American planes we were sure would be coming? Why did General MacArthur leave the Rock by PT boat in mid–March? Morale began to fall when the full effects of the fall of Bataan were realized.

One daily occurrence was the visit by "Photo Joe." Photo Joe was the name we gave the pilot of a small Jap reconnaissance plane that used to fly low over the water just out of reach of our machine guns at Battery Point. At the beginning, when we saw him approaching from the west our machine gunners would fire upon him, but the pilot kept just out of reach. After two or three weeks of frustration our gunners gave up. After that we would wave at him as he passed by, and sometimes he would dip his wings to acknowledge us. We knew that the pilot was taking pictures, but there was nothing we could do. I'm sure that his efforts helped the Japs because they eventually landed at the very spot where we had been bivouacked. They also attacked several other strategic locations.

Another frustration we all experienced on the Rock was the inability of our anti-aircraft ammunition to reach the Jap bombers that made our life miserable. We had no anti-aircraft ammunition that would reach the level at which they were able to bomb with effectiveness. So little effort was made to use what we had.

22

Just to keep us under cover, they not only dropped explosives but sometimes dropped blocks of cement or anything that would make us think they were real bombs. On one occasion they dropped bodies of Filipinos.

Sometime in February, one of our submarines brought in some new AA ammunition with timed fuses that allowed our gunners to reach the Japanese bombers' altitude. On the next day, when the Japs appeared as usual, our gunners opened fire on the two lead bombers. A shell exploded midway between the two planes which were so close together that the explosion ripped the inner wing off each plane, and they spiraled in opposite directions into the sea on each side of the Rock. Immediate cheers came from everywhere on the Rock. It is hard to describe the elation we felt as we watched the bomber that came down on our side crash only a few hundred yards off our beach area. A small boat was dispatched immediately to pick up one survivor (maybe the pilot) whom we could see in the water near the plane. In a matter of minutes, there was a Japanese fighter plane on the scene, and, after several strafing runs, he managed to kill the pilot, so our boat returned empty-handed. I had heard that the Japs would kill their downed aviators rather than allow them to be captured. To the Japanese, surrender was unacceptable. They would commit suicide (or murder) rather than surrender.

After Bataan fell on April 9, the Japanese quickly moved their field artillery pieces into hub-to-hub positions along the Bataan shoreline, and brought them to bear on our positions located on the side of the Rock facing the Bataan Peninsula. This action, together with the artillery pieces which had already been long in place on the Batangas side, put us in a position where we were caught in the middle. With the increased bombing runs, there was never a minute of the day when we were not under attack somewhere on the island.

After I got over the initial fear of falling bombs, I was less afraid because I was not in a place that the Japanese had targeted for bombing. While occasional bombs dropped nearby, the main targets were the big gun positions and fortifications. When the artillery started to pound us, however, it was a different story. The Japanese decided to soften up the beach areas for future landings. In contrast to aerial bombs, artillery shells were fired with deadly accuracy (because of a Jap observation balloon on Bataan).

From our positions we could see the Japs busily working on their artillery pieces in Bataan, moving and positioning and repositioning them to provide the best advantage to attack our gun emplacements. Their artillery was deadly accurate. They had German sighting mechanisms, the best in the world. If there was a redeeming factor for us, it was that generally only 25 percent to 30 percent of their shells exploded on impact. Many of them landed and then bounced up the hillside. Some of them broke open and spilled picric acid. Often some of our men could be seen coming out of foxholes and tunnels covered with the bright yellow powder. Everyone knew where they had been. We also knew how lucky they were to have been missed by the shells. Picric acid was not toxic but it was very sticky. A good shower and a change of clothes was the treatment—when and if one could do it, considering the conditions.

We learned that we needed to do two things to protect ourselves— listen for the sound of an artillery shell being fired and always be near our cover. We knew that when we heard the sound of the gun being fired we had only so many seconds to get under cover. Their firing patters were deliberate, and once they started firing, we knew where the shells were going (unless the first one got us).

There were two occasions when my area received direct hits with disastrous results. The first occasion happened only a few days after the fall of Bataan. It was noon and the portable kitchen was set up alongside the road just above the pill box command post. The Marine lieutenant in charge had his meal served at a table (unusual for the front lines), and he was eating when I drew my chow and started for my usual eating place. I heard the familiar sound of artillery fire from Bataan. I stopped in my tracks and made a beeline for the tunnel which was only about 30 feet away. Just as I hit the tunnel, a shell landed directly on the mess table, where the meal was being served, upsetting the two 50-gallon barrels of boiling wash water and boiling rinse water. Some Marines were scalded and everybody within 20 feet was killed. As soon as the shelling stopped, those of us in the medical aid station headed out to help the casualties and get them under cover. As the casualties came pouring into the tunnel, there were so many injuries that it was difficult to keep up with them.

When things cooled down, the Marine lieutenant charged into the tunnel and yelled at me, "Stamp, the next time I see you run like you ran into this tunnel, I'm going to shoot you." I was shocked and at a loss for words. I could only say, "Yes, sir." After I thought about it for a minute, I turned about and faced him and said, "Lieutenant, sir, I don't think I can keep from heading for cover when I hear a shell fired." He made no reply. Later, the medical officer reported this incident to the battalion commander, who came to our position to check it out. My thoughts went back to the night my friend and I were AWOL. This time I feared I didn't have a chance! Then the colonel arrived. He talked to

24

the lieutenant, with my medical officer and myself present. After he had heard the facts, the colonel, in effect, told the lieutenant that he would be a more effective officer if he would lead his men rather than push them.

That same evening, the Signal Corps brought out their search light and swept the water toward Bataan. They had been doing this for several nights at almost the same time.

They didn't realize that the Japs had a battery of guns trained on that light, and the Japs opened fire. They got not only the light, but several men.

When the casualties were brought into the tunnel aid station, I noticed a Filipino soldier standing nearby, literally covered with blood. He had the strangest wound anyone had ever seen. His head was sliced off sufficiently below the crown to expose his brain. How this man managed to not only walk to the aid station, but stand up until he got to us, I'll never know. He was dead within minutes after he arrived.

I never ceased to be amazed at the gruesome injuries produced by the violence of war: heads blown off, arms and legs severed, organs ripped out and torsoes cut cleanly in two, as if a surgeon had done it. Those were the physical wounds. If shock set in, the suffering was not so bad, and if death followed quickly, the individual was lucky. In my opinion, it is the psychological effects of war which produce the most suffering.

After being subjected to two hammerings by artillery on the same day, some of our outfit was moved out to another position closer to Bottomside, just above the cold storage plant, where we spent the remaining days of fighting on the Rock. This was just a few days before we eventually capitulated.

During the last few days; the bombing and the shelling almost never stopped. Our new location was just below several anti-aircraft batteries which were of special interest to the Japs, and therefore good targets, and we had several close calls. The most interesting thing that happened during those last few days was watching the supply truck trying to traverse the beach road between the cold storage plant and Malinta Tunnel. By this time the Japanese had several artillery pieces zeroed in on the road, and between the two ends there was almost no cover, except about midway, where there was a slight bank of about four or five feet. Several trucks had been blasted off that quarter-mile stretch, until way were devised to avoid the shells. One ruse the drivers used was to start from either end, travel quickly for about a hundred yards, stop suddenly, quickly retreat to cover from the artillery, wait until the shelling stopped, and then head across the open space at high speed. This strategy usually worked, but the plan had to be changed occasionally to keep the Japanese off balance. Another ruse was for two trucks to start out at the same time from opposite ends of the road, and both retreat quickly to cover, then one would proceed until the expected shells came in, then they would both race across the open road. Variations of this ruse were tried, but eventually a truck stalled trying to shift into reverse.

I could see the driver get out of the truck and head for the shallow ditch alongside the road. True to form, the Japanese quickly sent two shells toward the truck, one going high, exploding on the other side of the bank, and the second one landing near the truck. There was a pause when no more shells were fired. My sergeant said, "Let's go, Doc." I grabbed my aid kit and followed the sergeant down the hill to the road. We tried to stay in the ditch by the side of the road to avoid being seen by the Japs, but just as we got to the truck the shells started coming again and we had to find better cover. As soon as the shelling stopped again, the sergeant climbed over the small bank in search of the driver, and I followed the ditch for a distance further on, but neither of us found him. The sergeant and I were both recommended for the Silver Star. (I was awarded the Bronze Star.)

On the night of May 5th, I walked from my position to Malinta Tunnel for supplies. The route took me over the same road the trucks had to use, and I was more than a little nervous. Worse yet, it was a beautiful tropical night with a full moon. It was so clear that I could see the Bataan shore, and I imagined that the Japanese saw me. I was listening very carefully for the sound of an artillery shell being fired, so I would have time to take cover, if necessary.

I got to the tunnel without incident, picked up my supplies and headed for the tunnel exit. At the exit I was stopped by a guard and was not allowed to leave. When I asked why, I was informed that the Japs had set out from Bataan in landing craft and were expected to land somewhere on the Rock shortly. I informed the guard I was the only medic in my unit, and I needed to get back with supplies. He then checked with headquarters and let me go.

The walk back across Bottomside was more scary now, knowing that the Japs were about to land. I didn't walk; I ran as fast I could back to my unit where I was much more comfortable. The remainder of the night was filled with worry. We had all been briefed on several occasions about what to expect if the Japanese did land—and it wasn't pleasant to think about. Many were sure that the Japs would take no prisoners. So what would we do when they got here? Visions of terrible things happening to us filled our minds during that night.

One of the more versatile and moveable artillery pieces on the

Rock was the 155mm howitzer. All the other artillery 12-, 14-, and 16-inch guns were permanent placements, which prevented them from being used to help in Bataan during the fighting there. The 155mm's, however, could reach Bataan, and were very mobile and were used effectively along the Bataan lines. They were also the prime target for the bombing and artillery attacks. It was not good to be near one of their positions because they never failed to come under enemy fire whenever they were used. Unfortunately, they were fired and moved, fired and moved, and we often found ourselves near a gun battery without knowing it.

On the night of May 5, we were anxiously waiting when we heard the 155mm's overhead, obviously in answer to the Japanese landing forces, who had already been underway from Bataan when I left the tunnel. It was comfoting to hear those 155's because it meant that we were doing something, and not just waiting for the enemy to land.

We learned later that a sizable Japanese force had left the Bataan beach heading toward the tail end of Corregidor. When they were well underway, our 155's opened up on them, laying a curtain of fire *not in front of the Japs*, but *behind them*. The strategy worked, because our 155's barrage convinced them that they were being intercepted—that the Americans had just missed on the first salvo. The Japanese panicked and headed back to the beach. As they retreated, the 155's kept up their fire, only this time behind the Japs, decimating a confused enemy landing attempt. When they discovered what was happening, the survivors turned back toward Corregidor only to run into another 155mm barrage, creating more havoc. In the melee the Japs finally headed back to Bataan.

CHAPTER 5

It was inevitable that the Japanese would make a successful landing, and they did so in the early morning hours of May 6. During that day and through the next night the fighting was vicious on the small narrow tip of the Rock called Monkey Point.

A number of Japanese had infiltrated the Rock during this fighting. Suddenly people in areas away from the trench fighting were being fired upon. On one occasion people from Malinta Tunnel were getting some fresh air just outside one of the tunnel's entrances when the crack of a rifle sent them scurrying for cover. There were no sun breaks after that.

Closer to the actual fighting, on the opposite side of Malinta Tunnel from my position, there was a large water storage tank. It was a little way behind our lines, but it did command a view of the trenches. One of our hospital corpsmen was in the area, just beneath the tower caring for some wounded Marines, when he was drilled with a shot through the back of his head. A Marine gunnery sergeant who saw the whole thing immediately headed for the water tower, climbed up the ladder, and blasted the sniper off the tower. As he stood up on the tower to take a look, he himself took a round from another Jap sniper, and he died there. He was still there three weeks later, after we had surrendered. I was to learn later that this sergeant's defense of his hospital corpsman was typical of the Marine Corps' respect for their medics.

Our position overlooking the cold storage plant was fairly quiet in comparison to other places on the Rock, since the major action was concentrated on Monkey Point where the Japanese had established a beachhead. It was quiet, that is, until the early morning of May 7.

That morning the bombing runs resumed, and strafing was intense. Suddenly, there was the familiar sound of enemy artillery fire from the Mariveles shore, and everybody headed for cover in our small, but adequate tunnel.

Sergeant Major Russell stayed in a small lookout on the ridge above the Command Post, doing some paperwork. The first shell landed very close to his position and destroyed his lookout position. He was critically wounded. With shells landing all around us, two Marines brought the sergeant major into the tunnel, where several other wounded men had been brought.

While this was going on, I discovered that I had left my aid kit hanging on a tree limb outside the tunnel entrance. I had been using supplies from other kits and their supplies were getting low so I had to get my own kit. As I reached up for the kit, I felt a stinging sensation between my left thumb and forefinger. I looked up to see what had happened. There was a hole through the hand and I knew it had to be shrapnel. There were two tiny holes and bleeding was slight. I was surprised that I didn't hear the explosion of the shell that must have landed quite close.

When I got to Sergeant Major Russell, the first thing I saw was that he had a sizable chunk of flesh out of his right buttocks, deep enough to see the hip joint. He also had a serious wound of the upper right arm. He was in shock and there was very little bleeding. I packed the buttocks wound with a large gauze pack, and turned my attention to the arm. I found that his arm was hanging only by the skin. It was almost totally severed. I knew that there was nothing more I could do, except to watch for the shock to wear off. Next I cut through the skin holding the arm, removing it so he would be more comfortable. That was all I could offer him. I decided to hold the morphine because, at the time, he was in deep shock and did not show signs of pain. The company commander asked me about morphine for him, and I explained why I withheld it. I also told the major that I didn't think he would live an hour. The major accepted my explanation. The sergeant major was dead within 15 minutes. His loss was a severe blow to those who served with him. He was extremely well liked and respected by his superiors as well as those he commanded. he was the epitome of the Marine Corps.

While all this was going on, we got word that we would surrender at 1200 (noon). We were instructed to take the firing pins out of all the rifles and throw them into the bay. We had no artillery so our job was easy in that respect. I learned later that most of the big guns were loaded for firing, then the muzzles were packed with sandbags. When they were fired, it rendered them permanently inoperable.

From the time we were notified that surrender was imminent, there was a great feeling of depression. Hardly anyone had much to say, so I welcomed the opportunity to keep busy. It made things a little easier. I was busy taking care of the wounded, but I was scared. I didn't know what to think. Would they kill us, as several thought they would? (I couldn't help thinking about the Jap bomber pilot who was killed by his own people.) Would noncombatants (those not directly involved in combat, such as medical personnel and chaplains) be treated like all the rest? The more I thought about our situation, the more worried I became. After hearing about the Japs fighting in Bataan, I wasn't sure whether the red cross on my shirt would represent anything other than a target to the Japs (as had been reported).

An eerie silence descended on the Rock as we began to cautiously leave our shelter. The shelling had not resumed after the direct hit on our position earlier, and the bombing had ceased. Just as we were getting comfortable being without cover and knowing it was well after 1200 (noon), a Japanese fighter zoomed low over our position with guns ablaze. Once again we ran for cover.

After a short while, we felt that the strafing was an isolated case, so we began to make plans to assemble in front of the tunnel, while some men dug a hole and buried the sergeant major.

As soon as things settled down a little, we were able to move some of the wounded outside. The company commander then called us to attention and gave some instructions in preparation for meeting the enemy when they came. We knew that they had landed in several places on our end of the Rock. Instructions had been coming in by radio from the Command Center (in Malinta Tunnel). At least we knew we were not alone.

The major's instructions included what we could say, such as name, rank and serial number. We were not to volunteer any information about anything, regardless of the questions asked. We were also instructed to gather all of our personal possessions together and place them on the ground in front of us when we lined up for review by the enemy. It was strangely quiet as we waited with no small amount of anxiety. It is very difficult to try to describe the prevailing feeling at this time. However, one thing was very clear—all of us were together in this thing. Not one of us would be alone. This was typical of the spirit of the Marine Corps. When I realized that I was not alone, I felt much better. I believe that this comraderie was responsible for my ability to withstand the rigors ahead.

After an hour or more, we heard sounds of movement above and behind us, and in a short time a detachment of Japs rounded the corner near our position. A Japanese fellow who appeared to be the officer in charge approached our company commander. As he did so, one of the enlisted Japs went over the area with a flame thrower, burning everything that looked like it could hide something. The Japanese soldier was the smallest soldier in the group. He was not much bigger than his flame thrower. It was almost humorous to watch that little guy going about his business as if he enjoyed it—and I'm sure he did.

These Japs dressed differently from the soldiers that had been seen in Bataan and on the landing area on Monkey Point. It turned out that they were members of the JNLP (Japanese Naval Landing Party), the equivalent of our Marines. They were efficient, no nonsense, well trained, and they provided a marked contrast to the Army troops that we were destined to know. Looking back on that day, I feel that we were fortunate to be met by the better of the Japanese troops.

When the Japanese officer concluded his talk with the major, he started down the ranks, stopping in front of each man, getting a salute from each of us as he approached. Behind him, in single file, his men did the same thing, facing us and getting a salute.

That was where the similarity ended. Each Jap soldier then proceeded to search every man, looking, not for guns, but for rings, watches, money, or anything of value. This, we learned, was only the beginning of a long period of similar behavior.

I was at the very end of the line and watching what was going on, and I was shaking so badly that I was afraid I would show it. For some unexplained reason though, when he got to me the Jap officer received my salute, looked down on the large medical trunk with its large red cross on the top, turned on his heels and started down the road to the next position. Fortunately his men followed him, and I was spared, at least for then.

I really felt fortunate after they left. The reason was because of what was in the trunk. As we had been collecting our personal things for display to the Japs, I found that there was much more room in the trunk than I needed for medical supplies. Some of the men, noting that I had the room, asked if they could put their cigarettes, and some personal items that escaped detection. It never dawned on me that the Japanese would be looking for cigarettes, so I consented. Later, when

I finally opened the trunk, in Malinta Tunnel, I was surprised to find, not just cigarettes, but a lot of cash.

We had been told earlier to turn in our money to Command Center, but few did so. I turned the trunk and its contents over to the Medical Detachment headquarters.

Shortly after the Jap detachment left our position, I got back to the wounded who had not been picked up earlier. There was one soldier who had a dislocated elbow, and I could not get it into position to reduce the dislocation. He was in extreme pain because I had no morphine left. Since we had no orders or instructions, I thought that if I could get to Malinta Tunnel, I could get some medical supplies and bring them back to our position. I talked this over with the major and he not only agreed, but said that I should take some wounded with me. So I asked for volunteers to carry the only stretcher we had, together with the medical trunk. I chose to take the man with the dislocated elbow on the stretcher.

We started on our way, seven of us, when we met some Japanese soldiers at Bottomside. Two of the soldiers took a ring from one of the litter bearers and let us go on our way. We finally reached Malinta Tunnel without further incident, and that was the end of my freedom as I had known it.

CHAPTER 6

When I arrived at Malinta Tunnel with my work party, I was ordered to take my patient to the surgical ward, then report directly to the Medical Detachment Headquarters for assignment. The Marines with me were ordered to report to the 92nd Garage area, where all the prisoners were being assembled for shipment off the Rock.

There was so much confusion that it was a few days before I got an assignment, and that assignment was to a reserve unit of medics. The plan was to have an available cadre of medics that could be used when and where needed. I was told to report in daily until I was needed. I think the truth was that they didn't know what to do with me. By this time, the Japanese had set up their Command Center just inside the main entrance to the Tunnel and were beginning to bring some order to the chaos that existed.

Much of the initial confusion was caused by a deliberate attempt by the Japanese to break down our internal network of authority. They tried to do this by treating us all equally, without regard to rank or rate. This was the old adage of "divide and conquer." It was a challenge, but nearly everyone agreed that if we allowed this to happen to us, we would have less chance of survival. The enlisted men needed the officers to deal effectively with the Japanese. Without an organized effort, dealing with the Japanese would be impossible, and this is what the Japanese

United States prisoners in the Philippines captured by the Japanese (photo courtesy U.S. Navy).

wanted. There was general, but not total, agreement among those I was with that we needed to keep at least a part of our traditional lines of authority if we were to survive. Eventually the Japanese found that it worked to their advantage to allow us our own organization.

One of the first things the Japanese did was to designate an Army sergeant to be in charge of all Americans on the Rock. This Army sergeant named Roach (not his real name) had been an English teacher at a Japanese university, and a student of Buddhism. He had been in Japan for some years when the imminence of war forced him to flee Japan. He subsequently arrived in the Philippines just as the war started and was drafted into the Army. He wound up on Corregidor.

Because of his skill in the Japanese language, he was obviously valuable to the Japanese as a translator, but to put a man who had never even been in any military unit in charge of more than 12,000 military and civilian personnel was a sore that festered for a long time, not only among the enlisted men, but especially among the officers.

Sergeant Roach was allowed to set up a large space located conveniently near the main entrance to the Tunnel where he lived in relative comfort. Japanese soldiers had set up a command post near his office and kept guards posted there. The guards screened his visitors.

I stayed out of sight around his headquarters to avoid the guards.

34

One day when I was getting a haircut in the Tunnel, a Japanese guard walked by and chased everybody away. I got only half a haircut. Little did I know that that incident would be significant later.

Another time, when I was trying to be inconspicuous, a Japanese guard pointed to me and grunted something in Japanese. I had no idea what he was saying. Sergeant Roach saw this transpire and came over to talk to the guard. The guard pointed to the red cross on my sleeve and said something in Japanese, which Roach translated as: "You [pointing to me] are barber—he [pointing to the guard] wants you to cut his hair." I was scared to death. The only thing I could think of was that I didn't know how to cut hair, but I was afraid that not knowing how was just not going to be enough. How could I get out of this? The two conversed in Japanese for a minute, then Roach turned to me and said that the guard expected me to cut his hair because in the Japanese Army medics do those personal things for all the soldiers. "I'd do what he asks if I were you" he said, adding, "He will show you how." Roach then turned to the guard and said something in Japanese. The guard grunted back and produced a pair of hand clippers from his pack, holding the clippers as if he were cutting hair. I protested to Roach, but to no avail. He just repeated, "The guard will show you how."

I wound up following the guard to a place in a corner where there was a chair in which he could sit. The guard handed me the clippers and made that motion again. With shaking hand, I proceeded to cut his hair. It turned out to be easy, because he wore his hair clipper length, that is, like a crew cut. After I was finished the guard found a mirror, looked at the job I had done, then turned to me and motioned me to follow him. He led me out of the tunnel and across Bottomside, to the guard quarters. All the time I kept wondering what I was getting into. I was nearly petrified with fright. I had no idea what he wanted, and could not have understood if he had told me.

He led me into the barracks and pointed to me as he talked to some of the other guards. I have no idea what he said, but what he meant was easy to understand. He wanted me to cut his friend's hair. I wound up doing five haircuts, and afterward the guard gave me the clippers to keep. He then led me back to the Tunnel. I was still shaking when I got back and hunted for a place to be alone. There was no such place. In addition I had missed the evening meal.

To prepare myself for having to do the same thing again, I found a couple of the professional barbers and got them to give me some instructions. They agreed, as long as I didn't tell our guards that they were barbers. They wanted no part of it. To further avoid similar situations, I removed the red cross from my arm.

Meanwhile, a large number of men at the 92nd Garage were getting sick with dysentery, flu, dengue fever, and malaria. There were long lines of patients on litters being brought daily into the hospital. There was a severe shortage of food. Even before the surrender we had been on short rations, and now it was much worse. In spite of the food shortage, an arrangement had been worked out by Roach whereby the litter bearers would get extra rations when they brought patients in.

I was cutting Roach's hair one day when two Japanese guards approached him, engaged him in a discussion in Japanese, then left. A short time later, the two guards came back by our area leading an Army captain named Thompson out of the Tunnel. Captain Thompson was a veterinarian in the MAC (Medical Administrative Corps), and was the assigned mess officer at the Malinta Tunnel Hospital mess. Later, those same guards came back, said something to Roach, and abruptly left.

We later discovered that Captain Thompson had been unable to feed the litter bearers extra food for their extra work, as had been arranged, primarily because he didn't have the supplies. We later learned that the captain had been taken to an out-of-the-way place on the Rock, and it was presumed that he was shot by the guards because several people witnessed the guards leading the captain into an area behind a building, then they heard two shots. The guards came back alone.

An American Army officer had been shot by the Japanese for not being able to provide extra rations for the litter bearers. According to Pharmacist's Mate Second Class Irving J. Irvin (now commander, MSC, USN), Captain Thompson had refused to serve Roach some hotcakes he had demanded and had run him out of the mess hall, calling him an s.o.b. because he was making the same demands as the Japanese soldiers. There was no excuse for Roach to have acted as he did toward the captain. It taught us a valuable lesson. We dared not trust anyone, for fear of disastrous results.

The Japanese taught us another valuable lesson early during our incarceration. It was their policy to reduce rations for those too sick to work. This backward philosophy put the prisoners in a double bind. If they were too sick to work, they could not get enough food to get well and they would die. The end result was that many prisoners worked until they dropped, rather than try to live on reduced rations. For the Japanese, the policy resulted in more work days from fewer prisoners, but in the long-run, there were fewer prisoners to do the work.

Shortly after the execution of the Army captain, I was transferred to the 92nd Garage area, where the bulk of the prisoners were still assembled. When most of the men had been relocated to the 92nd Garage area, someone got the word that the Japanese and American

36

governments had made arrangements for our return to the States. Repatriation! Some of us were reminded how we were so optimistic at the start of the war. I heard someone say, "I told you so—it couldn't last long, now we can get out of this stinking place." For days nearly everyone kept an anxious eye toward the ocean, looking for transports that never came in. These kinds of rumors were to plague us for many months to come. The rapid rise and slow decline of morale caused by the rumors were devastating, particularly during these early days when no one knew what was going to happen to us. Throughout our stay, the most difficult thing we had to face was lack of communication from outside. Our internal communication was no better in the early months. We had no idea what was happening either locally or worldwide.

I was then assigned to a medical aid station, together with an Army doctor, Captain T.H. Hewlett, two Navy doctors, and three or four Army medics. I was the only Navy medic. A part of this medical unit was to stay on Corregidor with a 300-man work party.

There was a steady stream of men answering sick call at the medical aid station with a variety of ailments—beginning symptoms of malnutrition, influenza, and other upper respiratory illnesses.

There were still a number of men recovering from battle wounds who were experiencing a high rate of secondary infections. Such infections are a particular problem in the tropics because of the rapid growth of bacteria. It was particularly bad for us because of the lack of sanitation.

Sometime in July after my assignment to the medical aid unit, all of the Americans except the 300-man work party were moved to Manila by the Japanese where they would be directed to various labor camps by way of Bilibid Prison, where the Japanese had allowed us to set up a hospital, manned mostly by our Naval personnel. Bilibid had become a focal point for all American prisoners when being transferred to or from various labor work details. Nearly all prisoners, wherever captured, went through Bilibid at least once. While this was occurring, Army Captain Hewlett and Navy Lieutenant Glusman (both doctors) were assigned to stay on the Rock and provide medical support for about 300 Americans who were being kept there to provide labor for the clean-up of the Rock. The two medical officers were allowed to choose which enlisted men they wanted to stay with them. I was selected to stay with this detail. I had dreaded moving off the Rock to an unknown place so I felt fortunate that I had been chosen to stay.

When most of the prisoners had been moved to Manila, those of us who were to remain on the Rock were moved to a building that housed the old Station Hospital, located midway between Middleside and Topside. Most of the enlisted men were assigned to some large rooms

The old Station Hospital, Corregidor, in which POWs were housed in 1942–43 (photo courtesy Asbury L. Nix, former POW).

that had been hospital wards, while the officers shared some of the private rooms, usually eight officers to a room, with two-level bunk beds.

The enlisted men did not have beds, but with some ingenuity and scrounging around the island, were able to be fairly comfortable. There was a scant amount of electricity and running water.

Captain Hewlett and our medical unit were located in a portion of the building near what had been the mess hall. Some of the adjacent rooms were arranged so they could be used for the sick. One room was set aside as an aid station. Captain Hewlett convinced the Japanese Camp Commander that we needed a room for a separate surgical unit, and he gave us the mess hall space.

During the next few weeks, the Japanese allowed us to explore the island for medical supplies and equipment which might have been left in the various aid stations around the Rock, including the Malinta Tunnel Hospital. Sometimes the men would run into something useful while they were on labor details. The Americans and the Japs had long since removed any useful equipment from the Tunnel hospital, and even if we could have used any of it, the electrical power supply was not adequate to operate it. So we had no X-ray or sterilizing equipment. Nor could we find laboratory supplies and equipment.

We also needed a supply of linens for a surgical table cover, for surgical drapes, and for wrapping instruments for sterilizing. We did have some surgical gowns and a small supply of rubber gloves, surgical masks, and head covers, but we had no way of sterilizing any of these materials. Nor did we have a surgical table.

To solve the two problems—the lack of a surgical table and a method of sterilizing—Captain Hewlett found a round dining table about 6 feet across that had sturdy legs. He arranged with one of our men in the Japanese motor pool (the only ones who had tools) to cut the table top so that it would end up with a top approximately 6 feet by 2½ feet, with legs reinforced to withstand the weight of a person.

With the table problem solved, the doctor then managed to find an old-fashioned, oval-shaped, metal boiler in which water could be boiled to provide steam for sterilization. He then devised a wooden rack to hold the wrapped instruments up above the water level to be steamed. Then we gathered a supply of bed sheets, which some of the men had brought in from the former officers private quarters topside. These sheets were then cut into various shapes and sizes—some to cover the table, some to drape the patient, and the rest to wrap the instruments for sterilizing. While we did not have the most modern operating room, we could get by if an emergency arose. And it did—several times.

The kind of initiative and ingenuity shown by Captain Hewlett and other Americans was typical of things to come. The ability of Americans to rise to almost any occasion was never more manifest than during the time we were prisoners of the Japanese.

Meanwhile, our aid station served the medical needs of more than 300 American prisoners (and some Japanese) as best we could, treating mostly minor injuries, and the variety of skin ailments prevalent in the tropics. These skin problems were a bane to our existence. Infections, which developed from skin conditions, were a problem at first, but were better controlled as we were able to improve our sanitary conditions.

Upper respiratory infections were also a problem, since we had practically no medication. The sulfa drugs that became available just before the war started had all been confiscated by the Japanese, and antibiotics had yet to be invented. There was some malaria, but we had no antimalarial medications. Fortunately there were very few problems with malaria, which can be devastating without treatment.

One of the early developments, shortly after our work group had been settled in our barracks and the routine had been established, was the Japanese proposal to allow the prisoners the use of a brothel that was being set up for the Japanese soldiers. It was an interesting proposal, and I'm sure that some of the prisoners would have enjoyed the privilege, but the offer was turned down by Colonel Kirkpatrick, who was our official spokesman. I don't know what the official reason he

39

gave the Japanese was, but the real reason was very practical. The real reason was the health of the prisoners. It was well known (underground) that many Filipino girls were doing their bit for the war by giving their bodies, (along with gonorrhea, syphilis and related venereal diseases) to the Japanese soldiers. For any of us to get infected with a venereal disease would have been disastrous because there was no medication available. We in the medical unit knew firsthand that the experience of the Japanese soldiers with venereal disease was sometimes fatal. Some of the guards had tried (unofficially) to get Captain Hewlett to treat them for gonorrhea. He had no choice but to tell them that he had no medicine to treat them with. They would frequently confide in him, telling him what would happen to them if they could not get treatment. We knew that their soldiers who had contracted a venereal disease and become disabled were badly beaten, then treated, if medication was available.

To the Japanese Army, the sick soldier was as much of a handicap to their war effort as we prisoners were. If they treated their own soldiers that way, why would they let our sick continue to live? There were enough existing hazards for us already without contracting a venereal disease. This was a risk we could do without.

The senior American officer with our work detail was Army Colonel Kirkpatrick, an artillery officer and our official spokesman, who was very well regarded by the Japs for his valiant defense of Fort Drum (one of the four islands spanning the entrance to Manila Bay). Thus he was provided some special privileges. One of those privileges was a large electric fan mounted on a floor stand. One evening after work, on a particularly hot day, he showered, then lay down on his bed (he had his own room), turned the fan on, and fell asleep. The next morning he had a temperature of 107 degrees. I was ordered to give him tepid sponge baths continuously, while forcing fluids orally. Despite our efforts, the colonel died that afternoon. Pneumonia was probably the cause of death, but without X-ray or laboratory tests, it could not be confirmed.

The Japanese allowed Colonel Kirkpatrick's body to be taken to Bottomside for cremation. There he was placed atop a huge pyre on the beach. We were allowed to attend the ceremony (under guard, of course). One man was able to sneak an American flag onto the pyre by putting it under the body. Fortunately, the guards did not discover the flag, or trouble would have followed. This flag burning was justified.

The colonel's death was the second among our 300-man work detail. The first death occurred only a couple of days after we had arrived at our new location. An Army private was found unconscious and breathing with great difficulty. Captain Hewlett was called; he took a quick look at the man, pulled out a pocket knife (which the Japanese had not confiscated), made an opening in the trachea, then pulled an old-fashioned fountain pen from his shirt pocket, took off the cap and inserted the barrel into the trachea, securing it with bandages. Within an hour the man was dead. It was too little too late. The likely cause was diphtheria, which sometimes causes skin patches in the throat to slough off and clog the trachea opening. The private was taken out by a burial detail and buried in an unmarked grave.

Captain Hewlett performed more than 40 major surgical procedures without complications during the year the surgery unit was in use. This was a remarkable accomplishment, considering the conditions. At least two of the surgeries were performed on Japanese guards, under the watchful eye of the Japanese brass. I think that nearly all of the surgeries were appendectomies, and if not performed, might possibly have resulted in peritonitis and, more probably, death.

While Navy Doctor Glusman was with us, he would administer the anesthesia by drip method via ether mask. Then, when the patient was under enough, he would step around the table and assist the surgeon with retractors while I attended the drip anesthesia on demand. After Doctor Glusman left the Rock, I gave the anesthesia and helped with retractors, stepping back and forth as needed. The speed with which the surgeon worked allowed for a minimum of anesthesia hangover.

Meanwhile, the shigoto (work) detail had settled into a routine that consisted of a breakfast of boiled rice, called lugao. We received approximately half a canteen cup. Then there was tenko (muster) at 0700 (7 AM). Next, in groups of ten prisoners to each guard, we were escorted to the work place for that day. About noon the prisoners were led back to the compound for lunch, usually a cupful of steamed rice, and maybe a slice or two of some vegetable, and on rare occasions, a tiny piece of fish. Then came tenko again and the trek back to the workplace. About 1700 (5 PM) we were returned to the compound for a supper of steamed rice with a little vegetable, or fish, if available. For the rest of the day the men were free to do almost anything but leave the compound.

Although there were no fences or gates, the perimeter was watched carefully by armed guards 24 hours a day. The greatest deterrent to escape was probably the formation of the ten-man squads. The Japanese organized the prisoners in groups of ten for the purpose of maintaining accountability and discouraging escape (as if there was a place to escape to). We called them shooting squads, because the rule was, that if one of the ten men escaped, the other nine would be shot. That was a pretty heavy load to carry, but it became lighter as time went on. We learned to trust one another, although one could never be really sure if one of the others should decide to escape. There was a kind of understanding that, if one person should decide to escape, he would tell the rest and they would go with him. This threat was never carried out on Corregidor because there were no escapes. At Cabanatuan, however, there were several executions for attempted escape.

After a couple of months we became accustomed to the routine, but not to the food. Having already been on short rations for the last two months of the war, the rice diet did not help matters any. Many of us had lost 25 pounds or more. Those who had been on Bataan had lost even more.

Things began to change in September when the Japanese decided to pay us. It was their way of compliance with the Geneva Convention rule (which they did not sign!) on the treatment of prisoners of war. The pay scale was to be about the same as our Japanese military counterparts, *only in occupation money.* I believe the pay scale was: 15 pesos a month for privates, 30 pesos for sergeants, 80 pesos for lieutenants, and on up for senior officers. The officers were required to pay back 60 pesos a month to the Japanese for board and room. This put the actual pay rates for the junior officers about on a par with a sergeant's pay.

The Japanese had set up a store near Bottomside for the Japanese soldiers. By negotiations with the Japanese, Colonel Kirkpatrick had been able, in the beginning, to buy things from the store for prisoners. Since there was a limit on almost everything we wanted, a system of rationing was devised that prevented individuals from hoarding or getting more than their fair share. Accounts were set up for each man and records were kept to make sure that everyone was treated fairly.

At first there was some canned milk, canned corned beef (from Malinta Tunnel), peanuts, bananas, and occasionally sugar available, but as the items became popular with the Americans, the black market drove the prices out of sight.

In addition to the purchased food, some food items were found by the prisoners who took advantage of their break times to scrounge around the gun emplacements, particularly in Malinta Tunnel where there was still a lot of canned food items in hard to find places, especially corned beef.

These items were not available for everybody and, in time, became scarce. In the meantime, the Japanese were beginning to loosen up a bit and were allowing us to catch some fish. I'm not sure how it started but we were always trying the Japanese to see how much we could get away with or just how much we could get.

The Japanese maintained one of our old Navy launches at Corregidor, for travel back and forth between the islands of Fort Hughes, Fort Drum, Fort Frank and Corregidor. It was also used for Japanese personnel and supplies weekly between Manila and Corregidor. It was one of the same boats on which we had evacuated the personnel and patients from Canacao Naval Hospital, at the beginning of the war. In peacetime, I had been aboard one of those boats several times when going from Cavite to Manila for liberty, because it was easier and quicker than going by crowded roads.

A scheme to harvest fish from the sea began one day on one of the island runs. A Japanese crewman allowed an American to rig up an explosive device, made up of a brightwork polish can (a staple in the Army) filled with TNT and fitted with a cap and fuse. While fishing with dynamite was not a new idea to either the Japanese or some of the Americans, under our circumstances though, it was totally unexpected. The Japanese would benefit, however, as well as we did. So it was allowed for a while. The procedure called for one of the prisoners to toss the can as far from the boat as possible. When the charge exploded, a lot of stunned fish would float to the surface. Then we would all jump into the water and gather as many fish as possible, as quickly as possible, tossing them into the boat before the sharks appeared. It didn't give us much time, but the harvest was always good. To protect us from the sharks, an armed guard was always topside of the boat. I'm sure he was also there to prevent us from escaping.

With everything considered, malnutrition did not become a serious problem until early 1943 when the Japanese brought about 300 Filipinos to the Rock as a labor force. These ex-soldiers could not be repatriated because of guerrilla activities in their provinces. Then food became more scarce, security was heightened, and our scrounging was curtailed.

Several interesting things happened that I will never forget. From the very beginning, men who were listed as sick by the doctor would be excused from work that day, but I was required to replace them. This allowed me some experiences I never would have had otherwise even though I dreaded the work.

Once, when I worked for two or three weeks on the same shooting squad, I discovered a situation that became very annoying. It had been standard practice to carry a canteen whenever we went on the island because water was scarce in some places. At work, it was practice to hang our canteens in the shade on a tree branch nearby. When break time came, some of the canteens would be empty. Being without water in the tropical sun is miserable. Then one day someone happened to see our guard standing behind a tree drinking from one of the canteens. We had found the culprit, but what could we do about it?

43

That night I talked with Captain Hewlett about this problem, but the only solution we could come up with was for each man to keep his canteen with him all the time. Then one night I happened to think that maybe we could put something in the water to make it taste bad. I discussed this with the captain, and the only thing we could come up with was some chloral hydrate, which we had in the medical chest. Using such a drug had some risks, we knew, but the taste and odor was so bad that we figured that he would not drink it. What we did know was that the drug was commonly used in alcoholic drinks as knockout drops.

It had come to the point that we were desperate because carrying our canteens with us while we worked was too cumbersome. In addition, the water was always warm. I felt that it would be worth the risk if I could teach the guard a lesson. So, on a certain day, I put some of the drug in one canteen of water, and filled a second canteen with good water. That day I carried two canteens with me. Putting the drugged one in the usual place, I kept the other one with me. Everyone was told to keep their canteens with them. We didn't have to wait too long, only about an hour, but to me it was the longest hour. It was just before yasumi (rest) time when the guard walked over to the tree where I had hung the drugged canteen, lifted it off the tree limb, then proceeded to drain the canteen. My heart started to race, but I kept on working so I wouldn't watch him. Within a few minutes, he sat down by the tree (something no guard ever did), and in a few more minutes he was out cold. No one knew about what I had done so no one could point a finger at me, but they knew something was wrong. Anyway, the deed was done! When Yasumi time came, we all rested for awhile, then went back to work. We knew it was quitting time when we heard other details returning to our quarters, but our guard was still out cold. We mustered into a group and proceeded to return alone. When we got to the quarters, a guard asked us where our guard was. Our leader pointed to where we had been and then said, "Yasumi, yasumi" and pointed in the direction from which we had come. Within a short time there was a fully armed squad heading out. They later came back with the guard and his rifle. We didn't see him again until the next day.

This particular guard was called "Big Stupe" because he was. He was a particularly bothersome person, always hanging around our quarters, butting into our activities when we were off work, and we couldn't get rid of him. He knew just enough English to be dangerous. When he was around we couldn't talk freely, or do things we usually did when the guards were not around.

The day after the canteen episode, Big Stupe came into our

quarters as usual. He was very subdued, not like he usually was. He was visibly shaken and told us in his broken English, "me go New Guinea—me go back New Guinea." We knew that he had been there when the Americans took a part of New Guinea from the Japanese. He used to enjoy telling us about one battle with American Marines. According to him, he had faced one of them in hand-to-hand fighting, bayonet-to-bayonet, when the American Marine kicked the gun out of his hands, then kicked him in the testicles. Then, when he doubled up in pain, the Marine kicked him in the head. As he lay there on the jungle floor (acting dead), the Marine ground his foot in Big Stupe's face. "Americans very damn angry," he would tell us. I had listened to that story before, and I felt he was sincere—stupid but sincere.

Our guards were mostly men who had been on the front for a long time and were rewarded with easy duty. When Big Stupe told us he was being sent back to the front, we had a difficult time keeping from laughing. I, personally, felt much relieved after the episode of the previous day. There was no hint of what happened, so I began to breathe easier. Captain Hewlett also felt much better. He was the only other person who knew what I had done. I felt that I had done something to help make life a little easier for all of us.

CHAPTER 7

In January of 1943, food was still a problem. We had caught and eaten nearly all the iguanas and some of the monkeys. There was still one animal left on the island after all the bombing and shelling. Getting this animal would mean meat in our bellies for a change. After several tries, our senior officer finally asked the Japanese if they would shoot it for us, and they agreed. So the camp commander took some guards, the senior American officer, and a few selected men from the prisoner group and set out to hunt. When they found the animal the Japanese officer drew his pistol and fired. The old mule just blinked his eyes and turned his head away. The American officer suggested to the Japanese officer that the pistol was not heavy enough. He suggested a rifle. So the Japanese officer borrowed a rifle from a guard, thought for a minute, and handed the rifle to the American officer and told him to shoot. Responding quickly, the American dispatched the mule, and the men skinned and dressed out the animal. When the job was finished, Captain Hewlett was handed a solid piece of red meat at least a foot square and a foot thick. The good doctor always shared everything with his staff, and it was the best meat I have ever eaten.

One of the most important lessons we learned was to avoid, at all costs, humiliating or embarrassing the Japanese. "Losing face" was one of the worst things that could happen to an Oriental, and it was particularly serious to the Japanese, who felt that they were far superior to us.

"Loss of face" was involved in one incident that I remember observing. While we were on a work detail near Middleside one day, a member of our shooting squad did something that caused the guard to become angry. The American was a very tall blond man and the Japanese was unusually short, so the guard ordered the American to stand next to a large log nearby facing him. The guard then proceeded to climb up on the log, face the American, and let go with a vicious backhand at the taller man's head. As the guard swung, the American ducked his head quickly away from the swing. The swing caused the guard to lose his balance and he fell into the open arms of the American, who promptly dropped the guard on the ground. Enraged, the guard quickly got up, reached for his rifle, and proceeded to work the poor American over until he was nearly unconscious. I had never seen such a beating in my life. Those of us who had been tempted to laugh when the guard fell were glad we didn't.

Sometime in March or April of 1943, some Jap soldiers brought an injured American prisoner into our aid station. The American was a volunteer worker on a monument being built for the Japanese heroes in Bataan. He had been carried several miles through the jungle, and traveled by boat from Mariveles to Corregidor, rather than to Manila, because of the reputation of the "American doctor on Corregidor." To make matters worse, the man had suffered a fracture of the femur, a condition for which we had no treatment. He needed to be in traction, and we had no materials. Traction would consist of metal pins through the knee and ankle, to which ropes could be attached to pulleys and weights attached to the ropes. This steady pressure would keep the broken ends of the femur aligned so they could heal.

Captain Hewlett argued that he could not treat the American and that they should take him to Manila where he could be treated properly. The Japanese refused that solution and insisted that the doctor treat the man right there.

Several days elapsed before Captain Hewlett finally found a possible solution to the problem. For metal rods to put through the knee and ankle, he asked for and got, a spoke from the wheel of a Japanese bicycle. The spoke had to be cut in half, and one end of each half was flattened while the other end was sharpened to a point. The pieces were then sterilized ready for use. Meanwhile Army Lieutenant Goldsmith (from the motor pool) built a frame to place over the patient, over which the ropes could be placed so that weights on one end of the ropes could provide a steady tension on the metal rods.

When the metal rods were sterilized, and the patient made ready for the procedure under local anesthesia, Captain Hewlett screwed the pointed ends of the metal rods through the appropriate bones using an ordinary hand drill. After the metal rods were in place, the doctor attached small ropes to the rods, ran them over the frame and attached small weights to the rope ends. For weights, he used some scrap metal that approximated the weight he needed, starting out with a small weight and adding weight as traction needed to be increased.

This episode was typical of the ingenuity and adaptability of Americans, and in particular, one American. There are many stories about this American doctor. He did so many impossible things under such adverse conditions that he was a hero to us, as well as to the Japanese.

Another, more humorous event, took place in late 1942. Lieutenant Wright (the mess officer) felt inclined to have an appendectomy. His reasoning was that he had seen enough emergency appendectomies and realized that those men were lucky to have the facilities and the skills of a competent surgeon. This situation might not always be available. The good doctor agreed to perform the surgery, even though the circumstances were unusual, and it was done without incident. After he closed the surgical wound, Captain Hewlett, as an afterthought, decided to autograph the work and proceeded to carve his initials THH next to the incision. Years later they discovered each other's whereabouts and corresponded. Captain Hewlett saw Wright's name on a publication and wrote, asking him if he was the Wright on whom he had done an appendectomy in 1942. The general wrote back saying that he was, indeed, one and the same, asking Captain (now Colonel) Hewlett if he knew that there was a complaint filed against him for defacing government property? That was the general's way of kidding the doctor, for whom he had great respect.

Late in 1942 I was the medic on a detail that was sent to Fort Drum to retrieve a large generator for use on Corregidor. Fort Drum was one of the four islands that formed the defense of Manila Bay. The fortification was a concrete structure, shaped like a battleship, atop a tiny outcrop of rock. Its huge guns faced seaward, as did those on all four islands.

The generator in question was located in the bowels of the quasi-battleship and would require a lifting rig, powered by a diesel engine brought over from Corregidor by Lt. Goldsmith. After several days things were ready and the motor launch to carry the generator was ordered.

The generator had been hoisted to the top deck with the same engine that would lower it over the side. With great care, the huge machine was moved to the leeward side of the top deck, and the donkey engine was moved to a location from which it could lower the machinery by ropes and pulleys down to the motor launch below. Everything went well and the load was lifted out over the boat. It started slowly downward and, as the load passed about the 30-foot level above where the boat should be, the boat was pulled into position under the descending load. Suddenly the load picked up speed and never stopped until it bounced off the launch into the water. The brakes had failed. There was a strange quiet topside, until one of the guards started yelling "Goddamn Americans" over and over, while brandishing his rifle menacingly. We had seen this behavior before and, no doubt, would see it many times again. We didn't mind the Japanese thinking we were stupid, as long as only we knew what had happened.

Another incident had occurred sometime earlier. We had been moving heavy artillery shells from Malinta Tunnel to be loaded on Japanese ships tied up at Bottomside. The work was slow and difficult. One day one of the American officers suggested that Army Lieutenant Goldsmith (of the motor pool) be allowed to rig up one of the trolley flat cars with a diesel engine, so that we could carry the ammunition more quickly and easily. Prior to the war, Corregidor had an electric trolley system to carry passengers and light freight throughout the island. The Japs had removed all the rails except those at Bottomside.

In a few days, the flat car was ready, loaded with shells, and started on its way down the decline toward the dock. As it gathered speed on its way, it seemed to go faster and faster, until it catapulted into the water. The brakes had failed. Americans were called stupid that time too, but we knew what happened. Lieutenant Goldsmith had also engineered the Fort Drum generator caper. There seemed to be no end to the Lieutenant's talent when it came to engineering.

A similar thing occurred sometime after the trolley incident. It seems that the Japs were still looking for ways to more effectively transport the heavy ammunition and guns to the dockside for loading onto freighters. The Japs knew that there was a huge crane in Manila which could be used for that purpose. The difficulty was that there was only one person who could operate that crane, and he was a Filipino civilian who had fled into the mountains with his family (as did many others, at the start of the war). But with their usual persuasive powers, the Japanese were able to coax the man out of hiding, and brought the operator and the rig to Corregidor. I was on the work party at that time, and while the crane operator was maneuvering a huge gun barrel one day, I caught my leg in a bad place, and the gun barrel hit my knee,

49

bending my leg severely. The injury bothered me the rest of my days in prison camp and continues to bother me to this day.

Within a few days after I injured my leg, the crane operator managed to get a big load off the pier and out over the water toward the ship, when suddenly the load became too much for the crane and it catapulted into the water.

One of the most gnawing problems continued to be skin diseases. Skin problems were persistent and chronic, often defying treatment, even under the best conditions. With marginal sanitary conditions, skin problems would become acute and sometimes disabling. One such problem was inguinal ringworm, by definition "a contagious skin disease caused by certain fungi, marked by discoloration and scaly patches of the skin." The word "inguinal" refers to the groin area or crotch, hence the common term "jock itch." It is a painful, miserable, aggravating condition, sometimes making walking difficult.

Captain Hewlett had read everything available on the subject, and found that we had no medication specifically effective except tincture of iodine, and that, if applied to the skin in a covered area, would blister the skin and, in some circumstances, make the condition worse.

One day, while I was going through a medical book called the Merck Manual (known in medical circles as the *Interns' Bible*), I read an excerpt on the subject. The article called for a diluted solution of phenol (carbolic acid) followed by a dilute solution of hydrochloric acid (muriatic acid). The phenol acted as an anesthetic to the outer layer of skin, allowing the muriatic acid to penetrate and act on the fungi.

I discussed this treatment with Captain Hewlett, but he was reluctant to try it.

Shortly thereafter, a party was sent to Fort Frank. Among the group were two men who had been suffering with jock itch. I was assigned to that work party as medic. Before I left, I talked again with the doctor. He told me that if the men wanted that treatment, to take the medication with me and use it at my discretion. A couple of days later I applied the medication, as called for, to one of the men, and almost like magic, it supplied instant relief. So the second man begged me for the treatment and I gave it to him with similar results.

The next morning both men were incapacitated, with the whole inguinal region nearly raw. It was inflamed and weeping copiously. Neither man could work for the next few days. With strict sanitary precautions, the condition of both men improved and when we returned to the Rock a few days later, they were well. The best thing about the whole experience was that both men had no further sign of ringworm. There were no more volunteers for the treatment, however.

Just before Corregidor surrendered, the entire supply of Philippine government silver pesos, which had been stored on the Rock, had been dumped into Manila Bay to keep them from Japanese possession. The Japanese had heard of this huge cache of silver. They then arranged for some of our Navy divers (who were now in Cabanatuan Prison Camp) to come back to Corregidor to help recover the money. For weeks those divers worked at bringing up the silver pesos. The coins had been packed in boxes, and some of the boxes had already split open, spilling and scattering the coins. During the process of raising a box of silver coins to the boat above, the divers would open and scatter more boxes of coins to the bottom. The Japanese never got their money's worth in this deal.

In addition to spilling the silver coins, the divers would pack as many coins as possible in pouches sewn into their G-strings and smuggle them back to the Rock. Although the divers were quartered on Corregidor, they were not supposed to be in contact with our group, but it didn't take long before several of our group had possession of shiny silver pesos. The contact point was the motor pool.

The divers would then take the coins to the motor pool where someone would wash them with nitric acid to remove the corrosion caused by salt water. After the coins had been acid treated, they would be polished with Japanese tooth powder. (Many of us had no tooth brushes, so we didn't need the powder.)

At the time of this operation, a black market for silver coins developed. Through an intermediary, an American prisoner could write a check for $100 on any American bank, and in return he would get 50 silver pesos. This was a fair profit to the divers, if both the check writer and the diver lived. Considering what transpired in the course of events, I wondered what the collection rate was. This was only the first such black market operation that I encountered. I myself was later involved in Cabanatuan.

There are only two kinds of weather in the Philippines, good and bad. Three or four months of the year it rains almost continuously. (During the monsoon season in 1940, it rained 24 inches in 24 hours.) The other seven or eight months, a hot tropical sun beats on the earth during the day, and the temperature at night is uncomfortably cold. It was during the last weeks of the good weather, in the spring of 1943, that the Japanese challenged us to a baseball game. If the Americans won, the Japanese would reward us. Nothing was said about the Japanese winning.

Arrangements were made, and under the leadership of Army Lieutenant Goldsmith (motor pool), a work party prepared a field on Topside. Goldsmith also organized a team of volunteers (I was one),

51

and managed to get enough equipment together, with the help of the Japanese, to be ready for the game. A number of us wondered about what might happen if the Americans did win, would the reward be a day off work, or would the Japanese be angry?

Those who were to play managed to get some practice with a ball and gloves, but there were no places where we could get batting practice, except Topside, and that was off-limits.

Baseball was, and still is, a high point in Japanese society. Several of our captors insisted that the game was invented by Japan, just as they were sure that they had invented streetcars, radios, telephones, and the many other things Americans take for granted. We were in no position to argue, so they remained convinced. I remember seeing only two Japanese movies during those years in prison camp, and one of those was about baseball and love. The other was about the war, and showed a Japanese bomber pilot landing his big plane after he was already dead. I never ceased to be amazed about how little the average Japanese knew.

The day of the game was at hand. The Japanese insisted on a formal introduction to the game, and we went along with them (did we have a choice?). So the Japanese lined up on one side of a line between the pitcher's mound and home plate, while we lined up on the opposite side of the same line. After bowing to each other, the Japs took the field so they would bat last.

I had played a little baseball, but I was much better at softball. I wondered whether I could hit a baseball, but when the game was over, I had four hits, not because of skill but because I was so slow at swinging the big bat. They may be called sloppy hits but they count just as much as good ones. I was really proud of myself until someone told me that we were not trying to win. We did manage to lose despite my hitting spree.

A few weeks later the Japanese challenged us to another game. This time, though, we managed to eke out a close win. I didn't get even one hit. The Japanese were as good as their word, and gave us a 50-pound case of flour, with which Lt. Wright made some bread for our enjoyment. I believe the flour was part of what the Japanese had confiscated in Malinta Tunnel.

I referred earlier to an Army sergeant named Roach, who had been placed in charge of all Americans on the Rock just after we surrendered. He had been relieved of that position after Lt. Colonel Kirkpatrick had been named senior American officer by the Japanese. When our labor detail moved to Topside, Roach was given separate quarters, probably to avoid contact with the rest of us. He did not go out on work details, and the only time we ever saw him was when he came out of his room to pray to Buddha. One day he simply disappeared. No one missed him. After the war, I heard that he had survived the war, and had been tried in a New York civil court on charges brought by some surviving POWs. Apparently the court decided it did not have jurisdiction over military cases, and set him free. Those who sought justice were disappointed. He was one of only a very few individuals who disgraced the American name.

One of the things that most of us missed was a supply of reading material. I knew there was a considerable supply of books located at various batteries and other locations around the Rock, so I asked for and was granted permission to gather whatever I could find and set up a library wherever space permitted. Within a few weeks there were several hundred books catalogued and stored for the use of the prisoners. No one enjoyed those books more than I.

In the spring of 1943, the Japs brought a work force of Filipinos to the Rock. They were not prisoners technically, but they were former soldiers who were not allowed to return to their native provinces because of guerrilla activities there. They were officially members of the Greater East Asia Co-Prosperity Sphere, a political organization the Japs used to legitimize their takeover of greater East Asia. On the Rock they were not allowed contact with the American prisoners, except for Captain Hewlett and myself. I was permanently assigned to their unit for medical support, but I slept in my regular place.

Early on, after their arrival, there were some very sick Filipinos, and a few deaths occurred that were promptly reported to the camp commander. He apparently took this to be a reflection on the Japanese care of the Filipinos, so the camp commander told Captain Hewlett, "No more Filipinos can die." At least one more did die, unfortunately.

There is nothing the Filipinos enjoy more than a fiesta (a big celebration), and they will have one at the slightest excuse. When things leveled out for the new arrivals, the Japanese allowed them to have a fiesta. The Japs even allowed one of them to go to Manila on the boat run to get some food and liquor for their spree. The captain and I were both invited to the festivities and had a really good time. As we later learned, though, the Japanese camp commander had not been invited. There were some uneasy moments for a few days, but, as usual, the threat subsided.

A Filipino died one morning about 0600 a few days after the fiesta. I went to their quarters and verified the death, then proceeded immediately to the camp commander's quarters to report. I was a little uneasy because of the order he had given Captain Hewlett, so I wasn't surprised when I knocked on the door and heard him say, "Tell the man he cannot die until 8 o'clock." I left, returned at 0800, and reported the death.

When the Filipino work force had been well established, the Japs made preparations for the transfer of all the Americans left on Corregidor. Some of the Americans had been transferred off the Rock shortly after the surrender and had been transferred back for special reasons, like the divers had been. Those who had been out and back were helpful in telling us how to plan for the trip. There was a lot of advice, but little help because we each had our own priorities. Some concentrated on clothing, while others carried as much food as they could save or scrounge. I had difficulty deciding what would be most important to me, so I took a little of everything. I found a good Navy seabag, cut the top one-third off, reinforced the top and edges by sewing the raw edges. I then attached some straps so I could carry it like a backpack. I included two blankets, a mosquito netting, some underwear, my mess gear, and the clothes on my back.

On the appointed day we boarded a small ship at Bottomside, and proceeded to Manila. In Manila we were marched from the dock area to Bilibid Prison, which I had heard a lot about. I was hardly ready for what I saw there. This was one of the low points in my life, but it certainly wouldn't be the lowest.

CHAPTER 8

After we arrived at the dock area in Manila, we were marched in formation through the streets to Bilibid Prison, about five miles away. The streets were lined with Filipinos giving us the "V" (for victory) signs with their fingers, while trying to keep such gestures hidden from the guards. We had been told that the guards would not tolerate any kind of communication with the prisoners by the Filipinos, so we tried not to be too obvious in our acknowledgment.

Our guards were watching us to see that the Filipinos did not slip us anything, especially food. This display of loyalty was appreciated. Just by looking at those brave, unfortunate people along the route, we could almost see the suffering they had been going through.

Bilibid Prison had been a Federal prison in peacetime, but was in terrible condition from Japanese bombing and neglect. The three-story main building had no roof, but portions of the first and second floors were used to house various work parties as they were sent to, or returned from, work details. The prison buildings were arranged around a central large guard building, like spokes in a wheel. At the time we arrived, patients were housed in adobe brick buildings about 20 feet by 100 feet. There were separate spaces for contagious and psychiatric patients. The food was not as good as we had been used to, and there was more evidence of the effects of starvation diets here than on Corregidor. At

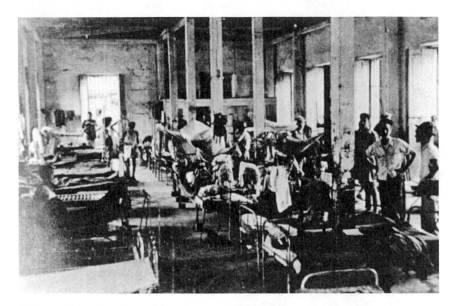

When U.S. dive bombers began to attack Japanese Naval vessels in Manila Bay, most patients in this hospital ward of Bilibid Prison were too ill to appreciate rumors that rescue was imminent (photo courtesy U.S. Navy).

Bilibid Prison Camp the medical staff (mostly Navy) cared for the sickest patients in the prison camp system. Those who were too sick to work on various work details were returned here to Bilibid for care, and if they recovered (which was rare) they would be returned to a work detail, after first going to Camp Cabanatuan, where food was a little better, until they regained some strength.

The majority of patients in Bilibid suffered from some form of vitamin deficiency, particularly vitamins B and C. The most common conditions were beri beri and pellegra, both due to lack of vitamin B complex, characterized by nerve damage and severe skin problems. Many of the patients suffered irreversible optic nerve damage (xeropthalmia) leading to blindness. Untreated beri beri victims frequently die of heart problems.

The lack of vitamin C causes a condition known as scurvy, or sprue, a miserable disease that leads to large blisters on the skin, external bleeding and a sore, burning mouth. It is easily prevented by fresh citrus fruits, but our diet contained no fruit of any kind.

There was an effort in Bilibid, however, to give some supplemental nourishment to those who needed it most. To provide more vitamin B, the medical staff maintained a large caldron of rice gruel, using yeast as

56

a fermenting agent. The gruel was then portioned out daily under the supervision of PhM2/C Bob Thompson, to selected patients. By adding more rice daily, a continuing supply was assured. The cost of this gruel was borne by everybody, in the form of a small decrease in the individual rations of rice.

For vitamin C, the medical staff was allowed to buy a small supply of fresh limes, which contain ascorbic acid and, like the fermented rice, was apportioned to those most in need. The effectiveness of these supplements was difficult to measure, often because it was too little too late. The patients who suffered most from avitaminosis were men who had been brought in from outlying work details where the nutrition was terrible, as was their treatment by the Japanese.

The sanitary conditions were fair. They were much better than when the prison was first opened for the American prisoners. I learned from several of my Navy friends that, at the beginning, there were only four water spigots for 8000 prisoners, and only two shower heads for bathing. The facilities for sewage disposal consisted of straddle trenches about six to eight inches deep leading to an open sewer at the exterior of the facility. Maggots were prevalent in all the drainage ditches. In addition to those health hazards, mosquitoes were a major problem. Rats, lice and cockroaches were abundant. By the time I arrived, however, sanitary conditions had been much improved.

For the improvement of the sewage system, CPhM Pliler, a sanitation technician, built a straddle trench, consisting of a metal trough about 10 inches wide and about 8 inches deep, with boards on each side for footing. The trench was built with an incline of about 15 degrees. Flushing was accomplished by a 50-gallon steel drum at the top of the trench, so placed that it was slightly off-center, and when it was nearly full of water, it would tip automatically, flushing the trench. Water came from a separate line and ran at a predetermined rate to avoid wasting water. The system worked very well and was a major factor in controlling the fly population. The only problem with this kind of facility was having to squat downslope from someone with diarrhea. There was always a race to get as high on the incline as possible.

One of the more pressing problems at Bilibid was the bad attitude of the guards. Contempt for Americans was obvious in every way. Yet, by contrast, it appeared that most of the guards were on the take. There were many stories of the prisoners bribing the guards.

While there were many instances of good things coming into Bilibid, in terms of some medications and food items, most of the things coming into the camp were the result of bribing the guards.

I discovered something going on at Bilibid that deserves mention.

One of the Navy hospital corpsmen had constructed a device with which he could duplicate a pill called sulfathiazole, made by Winthrop Pharmaceuticals. It was a drug that had been used successfully just before the war started, for the treatment of gonorrhea. As I mentioned before, a Japanese soldier who contracted the disease and became disabled was usually beaten. Sulfathiazole was thus important to the guards. Since the Japanese had long ago confiscated and used all the medical supplies, it was impossible for the guards to get any for themselves.

The device made by the corpsman consisted of a metal tube with an inside diameter the exact size of a sulfathiazole tablet. Then with a piece of bamboo carved to fit the inside of the tube, he would tamp down the ingredients to form a tablet. To make it more authentic, he carved a "W" (for Winthrop Pharmaceuticals) on the end of the bamboo, so that the final product was a perfect duplicate of the original. The only difference was in the composition. The copy was made of sodium bicarbonate (ordinary baking soda). The inventor must get credit for getting some medications and fruit for the patients with the money he got from the guards.

Morale at Bilibid was at a low ebb after more than a year of near starvation. Success in treating patients was minimal at best. It seemed like no one ever got completely well. The constant stream of prisoner work parties into and out of Bilibid left only the sickest people, and the death rate was extremely high, but it would have been much higher without the dedication of most of the Navy medical personnel, who continued to care for others, despite themselves being often as ill as their patients.

Most of the staff were Navy men and had been stationed at Canacao Naval Hospital prior to the war. I knew quite a few of them from the old days and was able to swap experiences since the surrender. I felt glad that I was not going to stay at Bilibid. It was too depressing.

There was one occasion while I was there that boosted morale for a while. The Bilibid compound had a high adobe brick wall completely surrounding the compound. It was thick enough to allow a walkway on the top, which the guards used to patrol the circumference 24 hours a day. Attached on the top of the wall were three high voltage electric lines, placed there to discourage anyone from trying to climb over the wall. It was not uncommon for the Japanese guards to stop occasionally to urinate off the wall into the clear area below. This practice made it impossible to enjoy the area outside our quarters. Then one day the inevitable happened with the electric lines. A guard stopped briefly on his patrol, turned to the inside of the wall and let loose with a stream of urine. Suddenly he let out a scream and pitched headlong into our side of the compound. He was obviously dead before impact. Everyone felt a little better for awhile.

In a short while we got word that our group from Corregidor was going to be transferred to another camp. At this point I think that most of us were ready to go. Almost anywhere would be better than where we were. I don't think that any of us knew then about Camp O'Donnell, where thousands of Americans and Filipinos died after suffering the infamous Bataan death march.

On the fateful day, we were loaded onto big trucks, packed like sardines, and headed for Cabanatuan, the largest camp in the Japanese prison camp system.

CHAPTER 9

Cabanatuan is located about 100 miles north of Manila, on Central Luzon Island. It lies in a large, fertile valley with a view of the coastal mountains to the east. It was one of the major rice growing areas on the island.

This third camp in the Japanese system consisted of a rectangle with four separate sections, a large hospital section on one side, and three sections for well prisoners on the other side of the camp. Two sections were for the Army prisoners, and one section for the Navy and Marine prisoners.

Between the hospital area and the well prisoner area were the Japanese quarters. The entire camp was surrounded by a tall fence fortified with barbed wire. Watch towers were placed strategically around the perimeter, and a clear area ten feet wide was maintained inside the fence for added security. The inside strip was patrolled by American prisoners.

The camp had been a Philippine Army training center prior to the war and consisted of about 100 wood and bamboo barracks with cogan grass thatched roofs. They were made of woven sawali or nipa strips. Framed panels on the building sides were hinged to allow for ventilation in the tropical heat. The interior of the barracks was arranged with two tiers of bunks with a surface of split bamboo. Through the central area of the 20 by 60 foot building was a walkway from end to end. Access to the upper and lower bunks was from the walkway. Each building was erected on stilts to avoid damage from ground water, since this area had been a rice growing area in peacetime. Drainage was always a problem and contributed much to the mosquito problem.

The buildings were designed to house 40 Filipinos. The Japanese crammed 100 Americans into the same space. There was a 29-inch width of sleeping space per man. In addition to the discomfort of crowding, the split bamboo sleeping surface caused ridges much like the surface of the old-fashioned washboard, sometimes causing bedsores around the hips, knees and shoulders. It is difficult to understand how healthy people could tolerate this discomfort. It was even worse for those suffering from dry beri beri.

When we arrived at Cabanatuan, conditions were good by comparison to what we had experienced in Bilibid. The food quantity was much better, but still not adequate for a working man, and it lacked nutritional value, especially protein and vitamins.

The camp itself and the buildings were fairly clean. Considerable effort was made to provide as good an environment as possible under the circumstances. This called for some discipline on the part of everyone.

The water supply came from a deep well and depended upon a diesel engine to pump it into a storage tank, which distributed water through small lines to the kitchens and to a couple of areas in each section of the camp. There were frequent failures of the pump engine, and we would be out of water, sometimes for days. With a scant water supply, baths were infrequent, and washing clothes was a problem. With good planning and some hoarding, however, we survived the problems in this camp. I believe that there was only one death for the first few months I was there. But that situation changed as we approached 1944.

Prior to the war the Philippine agriculture department had maintained an experimental carabao (water buffalo) breeding farm near the location of the present POW camp. The purpose of the farm was to develop an animal that would not only be a work animal, but one that could be used for food as well. At the outset of the war, the farm was abandoned and the animals released, subsequently scattering into the foothills nearby. On occasion, the Japs would allow men of the wood-cutting detail to kill and butcher a carabao. They would allow them to bring the meat into camp for the Japanese and the hospital patients.

One of the more serious problems of a diet deficient in protein is the body's inability to retain fluids. This causes frequency of urination. It was sometimes difficult at night to get to the pit latrines in time, so there was always a trail of dribbled feces and urine. This condition also caused problems for the men in the lower bunks. The more fortunate would cover themselves with a shelter-half. In the Army and Marines each man carried a shelter-half, any two of which could be combined into a small tent shelter.

Another, more serious, problem was beri beri. As I mentioned before, this vitamin deficiency syndrome is caused by the lack of vitamin B complex in the diet. There are two forms of beri beri with different symptoms for each kind. The wet beri beri caused retention of fluids in the body, particularly in the abdominal and thoracic area and in the lower extremities. This bloating was not as painful as the dry kind of beri beri, which in advanced cases, causes severe nerve damage. Often the nerve damage was irreversible. The dry type caused severe pain, in the legs particularly, to the extent that sufferers could not wear shoes, nor could they tolerate the pressure of a blanket, or any other cover on their legs. Those guys were really miserable.

Our doctors knew that the husk of the rice contained some vitamin B, and asked the Japanese if we could have unpolished rice for our diet. The Japanese approved this change and we started to get the new diet. Shortly after this change, the men began to have severe gastrointestinal problems, including bloody stools. After all this time on a bland diet, the intestinal tract would not tolerate the roughage and we had to go back on the polished rice again.

Life in Cabanatuan was not as comfortable, but it was better organized than on Corregidor. The pace was slower and there were efforts to keep the men involved in whatever activities they could, when they were not working. Checkers, acey-deucy and card games were standard fare for those of us who were handicapped (I was included in that category, since the injury to my knee on Corregidor).

After the walk in Manila I sometimes had trouble with my left knee collapsing when I stepped on uneven ground. There was no pain, but I fell frequently. Doctors at Cabanatuan felt that if I had a brace on my knee I could walk better. For this purpose, the doctors turned to an Army private who was talented in working with sheet metal. He designed a knee brace with sheet metal roughly contoured to the leg. He fashioned a hinged joint from the braces on an Army litter. It was crude, but when padded, worked fairly well, but not so well that I could work on the farm. I never worked on the farm, even when my leg improved.

The main labor force was used on the farm to work the land, which grew some vegetables that were sold in town and sometimes added to our rice. Another group worked daily cutting wood in the foothills, hauling it into camp for the ovens and cooking pots in the kitchens, one for each section. Still another work party hauled rice from the mill in Cabanatuan, to the camp storeroom. Both the wood working detail and the rice detail were to figure in some interesting activities that I will mention later.

I was assigned to the Navy dispensary. Our main function was holding regular sick call for men in our section and transferring patients who needed more care than we could give to and from the hospital.

One day someone came into the dispensary and asked if we knew the latest scoop. "Germany has surrendered," he said. The date was sometime in August 1943. I don't remember whether or not I had a bad day, but I reacted to this news in a negative way by saying something like "anybody who believes that rumor believes that we will have ice cream for lunch." The reaction was swift in coming. One of the hospital corpsmen, named Nelson, punched me hard enough to almost knock me down. I wound up with a black eye and a wounded ego. The end result of this altercation was that the Navy doctor sent me to the hospital, probably for psychiatric reasons. No one ever told me. I do know that I was tired of the rumor roller-coaster.

I was in the hospital for about a month when the hospital section was moved across the camp to what had been Army section 1. This relocation resulted in the hospital being designated as section 1. The rest of the old section 1 and the old section 3 were combined and redesignated section 2, while the old section 4 became section 3. This put all the American prisoners on the same side of Cabanatuan Camp for better security by the Japanese.

By the fall of 1943, there were several men who had underground connections with some Japanese guards to smuggle things into camp. We had been paid in Cabanatuan just like we had been on Corregidor, so there was plenty of money with which to buy things. The only limitation was availability. There were now two sources of supply. One of these sources was the official purchases by our camp leaders who could buy such things as eggs, peanuts, bananas, unrefined sugar, etc., while the black market provided such things as coffee and tobacco.

I personally got involved in buying coffee through a Japanese guard whom I never saw (my contact was another prisoner). I would buy a kilogram (2.2 pounds) of ground coffee, then arrange for the kitchen crew to make the coffee for me. This was done by boiling the coffee in 5 gallon metal cans on the kitchen stoves. In return the kitchen crew could help themselves to the coffee. At the beginning, I paid 5 pesos for the coffee and sold the prepared coffee for 20 centavos for a canteen cupful (about 1 pint). By boiling the coffee over a time or two I could make 20 pesos on a kilogram of coffee.

There were only a few involved in this kind of activity, but the extra money meant very little when there was so little to buy on the legitimate market. I remember one fellow who was desperate to make a cake when he got some black market flour. He discovered he had nothing with which to grease the pan. He had already prepared the batter and had the pan ready. After searching to see if anyone had oil, he gave up and used some shoe polish. Believe it or not, he sold most of the cake. What puzzled me at the time was why anyone would have shoe polish. I shouldn't have been surprised though, some strange things showed up in camp.

Shortly after the hospital had moved to its new location, I was discharged. Before I left the hospital, I made arrangements with an Army sergeant to join him in a barber shop in section 2. The senior officer of that section wanted barbers just for the officers of that section. So it was that I got back to barbering, which was the best thing that happened to me at Cabanatuan.

Somebody had already constructed a small building to serve as a barber shop. It included some wooden chairs with backs that reclined and fitted with what could be called a headrest, so that we could shave. I had become fairly good at cutting hair, but I had never shaved anyone before.

We needed tools with which to shave. We had hand clippers and combs but no razors. Knowing that razors (even safety razors) were forbidden, we put out the word. We knew there were some out there. We just had to find them.

It wasn't long before we had two instruments that we could use. There were no razors available (at least at that time) but one man had made a razor out of a butcher knife which he got from the kitchen. After cutting the blade to an appropriate length, he was able to put a good bevel on the cutting edge by putting an aluminum backing on the knife.

From the beginning, the barbershop was a good place to work. The sergeant and I both kept our personal gear in the shop (which we could lock), and slept in the barracks nearby. During the time I worked in the barbershop, I joined a quan group (a food sharing group) with a young civilian, who was an electronic wizard, and an Army private named Morton Eichner. Eichner was so debilitated by dry beri beri that he was unable to walk very well, so it was arranged that I would draw his rations and bring them to him. The three of us shared everything we could. During the year I quanned (a Filipino term for something that has no name) with Eichner, we played cribbage whenever we could, and we tried to keep track of how many games each of us won. He had a distinct edge on me in the several thousand games we played.

There was a little more ground space for us around the shop, and like a lot of others, we had our own little personal garden plot in which we planted such things as garlic, radishes and onions, which we used to flavor our rice. The officers would usually have some seeds for us, or we could trade a haircut or shave for seeds. Seeds came from the farm, where most of the men worked. Bringing anything in from the farm was forbidden, but seeds could be hidden easily.

The barbershop was a good deal for us for several reasons. I remember that soap was always in short supply, and sometimes we needed some for shaving, so we would trade a haircut for a bar of soap. When we had enough soap to put some away, we would boil the soap down until it was thoroughly mixed, then let it solidify again for storage. We would also trade cigarettes or tobacco for soap. Sometimes we would cut hair for cigarettes to trade for soap. We also had a deal with the kitchen crew who allowed us to heat water for shaving—for free haircuts.

In what I think was a fit of conscience, the Japanese decided to try to do something about the fly problem. Flies were everywhere, and they were hungry! They came mostly from the open pit trenches throughout the camp. These pits were terrible, and there were no chemicals to reduce either the fly larvae or the odor problems. How simple it would have been to use chlorinated lime. But the Japanese would not think of anything so easy, nor would they listen to the Americans who had experience in sanitation.

The Japanese felt that the fly problem could be controlled by killing them, not with chemical or sprays, but by swatting. So every man was ordered to kill and turn in 50 flies every day. Everybody enthusiastically tried hard to reduce the fly population. At first there were some setbacks. The first setback was to try to find a method of collecting and keeping dead flies to turn in. It seemed that no matter what was used to store the dead flies, the ants would devour them. A person would kill 50 flies, put them in a container, only to find that, when he went to get them to turn in, they had disappeared. The solution was to find an ant-proof container. Even then, sometimes the dead flies disappeared. Some of the guys were too lazy to kill their own flies, so they devised fly traps—which turned out to be the second setback. Fly traps would have been effective, except that there was no way to keep out the ants. I was one of the lazy ones, but I did not use a trap. The sergeant and I would charge 20 flies for a haircut, or shave. That deal would give us an extra supply of dead flies for insurance. We all soon found out that good tight containers could be fashioned out of the old Army first aid kit that used to hang from the rifle belt. The kit could also be carried in a pocket, if one had clothes with pockets. When the Red Cross packages arrived later, we learned that Nescafe (instant coffee) cans served equally well.

Sometime in the fall of 1943 it was announced that the American Red Cross had sent some packages to the American prisoners of the Japanese. The camp commander told us that they would be distributed in a few days. It was more than a few days, but distribution was made only after each package had been opened, and the Japanese had taken what they wanted — mostly cigarettes and candy. My package indicated that it had been sent from my wife. We later learned that the Red Cross had put the names of next of kin on all the packages. We never knew what happened to the thousands of packages sent to those prisoners who had already died.

The packages contained a number of items that were all welcome. There were shoes and socks, neither of which I had. There were various food items (not the same in every box). There were cans of Spam, corned beef, salmon or pate. There were containers of powdered milk, butter, cheese, sugar, and soluble coffee. There were chocolate bars or some other form of candy and gum. Other items included toilet soap, toothbrush, toothpaste, and cigarettes.

When the Red Cross boxes were all distributed (over a period of two or three weeks), trading was at a fever pitch: cigarettes for Nescafe or Spam, powdered milk for cigarettes, and any number of other combinations. When things got to be in short supply, the trading value would increase, decreasing the value of a haircut or shave for trading purposes. So much for the barber business. One of the most difficult items to trade became shoes. The closest I could come to finding my size was a pair one and a half sizes too large, but they were better than none. A few months later, I would lose those shoes swimming away from a sinking Japanese prison ship, the *Oryoku Maru*.

There were some civilians in camp who were reported to be operating a black market and taking checks written on any bank in the States. Obviously, few of the enlisted men had checking accounts, and I was not one of the lucky ones who did.

I referred earlier to those who were able to get things through the guards, either directly or indirectly (through an intermediary). Those who got things through the guards directly were referred to as brokers, and very few people knew who they were. Only a few tried the direct method. Such was the case of one Army medic in section 2, who used to crawl under the fence at night, go to a nearby barrio (town), and pick up medicines and food items that had been prearranged, then return to the camp and crawl back under the fence. Of course this could only be done with the aid of a Japanese guard. This went on for some time, until one night, when he had gone to the barrio, the Japanese guard was changed. When the medic returned, he was caught by the new guard. He was beheaded the next day, and his head placed on one of the fence posts for all to see.

Years later, when I visited the old Cabanatuan site, I stopped at the little barrio and talked to a Filipino minister, who remembered those days. He told me that several of the people in his barrio had been killed after the soldier was caught. One of those killed was his son.

From the start, brutality was common at Cabanatuan, but it was usually on an individual basis. What with the ten-man shooting squads the Japanese used to control escapes, there was little to abate the fear of that kind of reprisal. We were always aware of that kind of threat, and constantly worried that one of our group might decide to escape out of desperation, now that conditions were continuing to deteriorate.

There were a number of psychiatric prisoners in a special lock-up, and a few of them tried to escape. The Japanese were so afraid of these obviously insane prisoners that they always allowed us to handle them, and we would be allowed to go out with the soldiers to look for them. They were always easily found because of their confused state. One was found after several days, dead under a pile of weeds, where he had crawled, only a few yards from the perimeter fence.

According to some witnesses, three enlisted men escaped from Cabanatuan in July of 1942 by just walking away. Several hours later the men were returned. In front of everyone, the prisoners were tied to poles stuck in the ground. They were then tied in such a way as to cause the greatest agony. After about 18 hours, the men were untied, led to open graves and executed. Witnesses also reported that three officers, one a Navy ensign, escaped about the same time as the enlisted men and received similar treatment. In both cases, there were a lot of extremely scared men, but in neither case was the shooting of the other members of the squads carried out.

For awhile in late 1943, there was a lighter side to life. The Japanese allowed and, indeed, encouraged efforts on the part of the prisoners to find ways of entertaining themselves. To that end, considerable talent had been discovered among the prisoners. Led by a young Army officer, a Harvard graduate, who was experienced in drama, several skits were written and performed on a makeshift stage erected for that purpose. Props and other equipment were fashioned out of scrap materials.

Some of the more interesting entertainment included a jazz band featuring several members of the old Fourth Marine Band (from the Shanghai Marine detachment). The trombone soloist, an Army private, had been a member of the Glenn Miller band, when he was drafted just before the war started.

When the call went out on the underground system, a number of the instruments were contributed by Filipinos. There were two pianos, clarinets, cornets and guitars plus the trombone used by the ex–Glenn Miller band member. The one instrument not available was a bass drum, or bass viola for rhythm.

Using an old-fashioned wash tub (that just happened to be around) a suitable bass viola was fashioned by attaching a long wooden handle to the side, so that when the tub was inverted the handle pointed upward. A piece of strong carabao hide was then attached to the middle of the flat surface of the tub and extended upward and attached to the upright handle so that enough tension could be put to the hide string, when plucked, to produce a bass sound. Variations in pitch were made by increasing or decreasing the tension on the single "string." Years after the war I saw Caribbean musicians use this same kind of instrument. I don't know which was first.

The skill of the orchestra and the clever skits interested even the Japanese, who insisted on front-row seats at the performances. It was holiday time and one of the first skits this group performed was a take-off on Dickens' *Christmas Carol*, with a clever reference to our captors as Scrooges. At no small risk, some of the skits were clever spoofs of the Japanese. There was no reaction from the guards when they watched the skits, so we were never to know whether they approved of the spoofing or didn't understand the skits. Nevertheless we enjoyed them all. Our spirits were lifted for a time, and the performances did a lot for us.

Most of our guards seemed to possess the mentality of morons. They were known to us by such names as Donald Duck, Mickey Mouse, Web Foot, Air Raid and others. Donald Duck reportedly asked an American what the name meant, and was told that it was the name of a movie star. He was pleased.

I have referred to the things that the Japanese considered contraband in Cabanatuan (as they did on Corregidor and in Bilibid). These items included, but were not limited to, knives, razors, radios, American money, and miscellaneous items, determined at the whim of a guard or the camp commander. Inspections were frequent and unannounced. The Japanese would always start with a team of guards appearing at barracks #1, just inside the main gate. When this happened, the occupants would quickly lay out their possessions for inspection (each man had a pack just for inspections). From experience, those men learned that the Japanese would look for a specific item, and if they found that one item, that would be all that they looked for as they went from building to building. Since every inspection started in barracks #1, the men in the next barracks would be alerted by the signal "AIR RAID," that an inspection was in progress. By the time the Japanese got to the next barracks everyone was not only ready, but knew what the guards were looking for. Our spirits may have been lifted by the entertainment, but the frequent unannounced inspections and tenkos (roll calls) were upsetting.

During days that were slow in the barber shop, I often spent time with an Army lieutenant colonel, named Peoples, who was a very good amateur magician. He used to entertain us with his sleight-of-hand whenever there would be a small group, which was frequent. He used to show me how he did the tricks and was very patient with me as I learned a number of coin and card tricks, some of which I still remember.

At one time I ran a poker game at night for a Navy man who had a continuous operation, because he had to work on the farm during the day. The moonlight was frequently bright enough to read cards. He hired me to act as his dealer in a running poker game in an out-of-the-way place. My job was to deal the cards and rake in 5 percent of the pot, which I gave to him when he got in from work and could take over himself. One of the reasons I did this was because I knew him—he had been my boxing coach on the *Canopus* before the war started.

I frequently think back on those days with amusement. I remember having several hundred pesos (occupation money), and I could have had a lot more. In reality, I had nothing. There was nothing I could buy.

A part of the entertainment in camp, at least to me, was to sit in the evening and listen to some of the more talented people tell stories about their experiences. One of the best storytellers was a man who had been on active duty in the Army for more than 50 years. I spent many interesting evenings listening in fascination. He was in his seventies and seemed to be in good spirits. I never knew if he got home safely.

In addition to the chronic hunger and the misery of beri beri, scurvy, pellagra, and malaria, the flies, mosquitoes and bedbugs made life miserable beyond description. During the daytime, the flies got into our food to the extent that it was difficult to eat. They also made sitting on the latrine an almost unbearable experience. During the nights the mosquitoes' hum was so loud it almost kept one awake until, from sheer exhaustion, one would fall asleep only to be attacked by hordes of bedbugs.

The bedbug has to be one of man's worst enemies. It hides in the tiniest cracks in the woodwork (bamboo in our case) and can penetrate clothing, sheets, and even blankets to get to the source of warm blood.

Their bites cause hive-like eruptions at the site, and the itching is maddening. There is a distinctive odor that is very unpleasant whenever they are present. The only control we had was to subject our bedding and clothing to live steam. Periodically, we would be given a day off so we could fill some 50-gallon drums with water, build a fire under them, bring the water to a boil and keep it at the boiling point. Then we would take turns setting our bedding and clothing over the steam for 10 minutes or so. This provided only temporary relief because only the bedding and clothing were treated. The bugs remained in the woodwork and a new batch of bugs would attack as soon as someone sat or laid down on the woodwork.

During the early months of 1944, rations reached a new low for Cabanatuan. The black market had literally ceased to exist. Filipino farmers had quit farming because the Japs were taking all the produce and giving them nothing in return. There were frantic efforts to get extra food from any source possible. Stray dogs who wandered into camp were usually victims of our hunger. Cats, rats and snakes were also frequent food sources.

On one occasion two men found some corn cobs in the garbage. The men cut the cobs into tiny pieces and ate them. They next day they were both dead. It is difficult to explain hunger pangs that cause this kind of risky behavior. Hunger is a powerful motivator.

About this time the Japanese discovered a serious discrepancy between the amount of money they paid us on a monthly basis and the amount of money we were spending on purchases we were allowed to make legally. I don't know the amount, but it was reported to be three to one. For example the Japanese records might show that they had paid the prisoners 100,000 pesos, while our records, required by the Japanese, would show 300,000 pesos spent in the same period. The Japanese knew something was wrong but it took them several months to solve the mystery.

CHAPTER 10

By the middle of 1944, morale had reached the lowest point yet, and some of us wondered if it was worth trying to hang on. Thievery was becoming a major problem. Some, who would never steal ordinarily, were so driven by hunger that they could not help themselves. They were desperate, and desperation often leads to tragedy. We didn't need more adversity to test our strength. An air of depression permeated the camp. Things were bad, but not nearly as bad as they were to become later.

I mentioned earlier about the small personal gardens many of us kept. The little gardens were popular targets for the hungry. One incident I remember still was the confrontation of a thief by the owner of a small garden plot. The owner caught the thief in the act, stood him up (he was bigger than the thief), and hit the thief with such a vicious punch over the heart that he collapsed. It was dramatic, but hardly stopped the stealing. Most of us got along well under very difficult conditions.

One tragic incident involving personal gardens occurred early in 1944. It involved one of the civilians in camp. He was tending his garden which was located next to the 10-foot imaginary inside perimeter near his barracks. While working in his garden he stepped on the unmarked line, and the Japanese guard in a nearby tower shot him through the head without warning. He died instantly. It turned out that the man was the son of an ambassador of one of the Far Eastern countries. The senior American officer protested to no avail.

During better times in Cabanatuan, I received some money from an anonymous donor. I wasn't the only one to receive money through the gravevine. I now knew why there was more money spent in camp than the Japanese paid us. Nobody would talk about this situation in deference to the donors and the men who were directly involved in the situation.

One afternoon in late July or early August of 1944, there was a flurry of activity by the Japanese. The line of carabao carts coming back from the Cabanatuan rice mill was diverted at the main gate by Japanese guards and detained in the Japanese section of the camp. Normally the men would have gone directly to the storage area where they would unload the rice, put the carabao into the pasture area, and go to their barracks.

A short time later, the Japanese guards descended on our side of the camp, screaming at us and ordering us into our barracks. Something was going on. We did not know what. On their sweep through our side of the camp, they led several senior officers away to the Japanese side of the camp.

That same afternoon the woodcutting detail was also diverted to the Japanese side. When no one came back from the Japanese side that evening or the next day, we began to wonder what was going on.

On the second day information began to filter in that the Japanese had uncovered the smuggling ring that had brought contraband into the camp. For two years those brave prisoners had gotten away with bringing in large amounts of contraband at considerable risk to themselves. Their fate was now in the hands of the Japanese.

I learned later that the organization behind the operation included two valiant Filipino women, one known as "Miss U" and the other "Highpockets." Both deserve the highest acclaim. The organization used school children, primarily as runners for the contraband as it was moved the 100 miles from barrio to barrio to Cabanatuan. The children would carry the tiny packages in their lunch pails on the way to school each day. A contact at each school would be responsible for receiving what the children brought to school and arranging for the next move along the line. There were two destinations for the contraband: one was the Cabanatuan rice mill and the other was the forest area where the prisoners were cutting wood for the kitchens in the camp. When the contraband arrived at the rice mill it was hidden in the rice bags wich were delivered daily to the camp, where they were put in a storeroom in the Japanese area. The bags were then opened and the contraband taken into our side of the camp, where an unidentified group would take possession and distribute the materials in such a way that no one was identified. They did an excellent job, and the material was always equally distributed. There didn't seem to be any misuse of the materials. I believe that everything went to the person designated. It turned out that the internal organization was headed by an Army colonel named Oliver in the chaplain's corps. He was one of the real heroes of Cabanatuan.

Somewhat like the rice detail, the wood cutting detail received the contraband in the area where they worked and brought it into camp, hidden in the carts and wood. On arrival in camp, the cut wood was stored in sheds built for that purpose and located near the rice storage. From here the contraband was easily brought into camp and distributed as it was from the rice detail.

I never learned what happened to the enlisted men involved as carriers, but as far as I know there were no executions. The worst punishments were handed out to the American officers in charge of the two details. The two officers, one an Army lieutenant and the other a Navy commander, and Chaplain Oliver were sentenced to "hard" confinement, which meant that they were put into individual bamboo cages of such size as to prevent sitting, lying down, or standing—only permitting kneeling. Both water and food were withheld.

The cage was uncovered and the men exposed to the hot tropical sun during the day and the very cold temperatures at night. How long the punishment lasted I never knew. Watching those men in their agony was a difficult experience at the time. They were suffering for what they had done for all of us, and we had no way of even saying thank you.

The wards in the hospital were numbered consecutively starting with "0," or Zero ward as it was known. As patients were admitted to the hospital, they would be assigned to a ward according to the severity of their illness. If their condition improved, they would either be discharged back to their work units or assigned to a lesser care unit (higher number). If their condition worsened, they would be moved to a heavier care unit (lower number). The most intensive care was supposed to be given on Zero ward, but in reality patients were sent to Zero ward when doctors felt that nothing more could be done for them. The Zero ward personnel served on the burial details. They would pick up and carry the dead on litters to the farm where there was a large open, water-filled pit. This pit was about 30 feet long and 10 feet wide. As bodies accumulated in the pit, they would float on the water surface until decomposition was far enough along for the bodies to sink in the

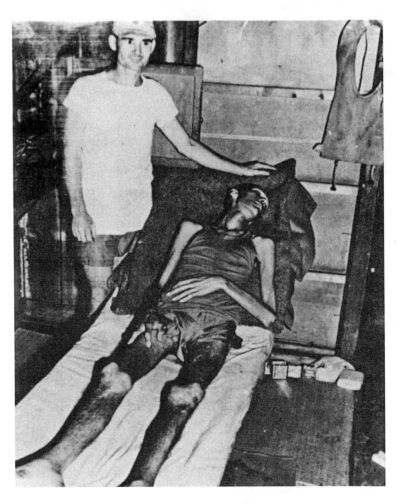

A gaunt U.S. prisoner of war from Aomori, Japan (photo courtesy of the U.S. Navy).

muck below. The stench was terrible. On the one occasion when I had to go there, I could not help being nauseated. In later years, when I think back on that experience, I'm reminded of the pictures of the Holocaust in Europe during World War II.

I shall never forget a miracle experience at Cabanatuan. I came to know the individual later, and I'm still amazed when I think about what happened. When conditions at Cabanatuan were at their worst, prisoners were dying in large numbers (sometimes as many as 20 or 30 daily). The hospital (at its original location) was struggling to care for very ill patients with very little in terms of supplies or equipment.

The miracle experience involved a young soldier of Native American heritage. He, along with several others who had been pronounced dead by the doctors, was taken from the Zero ward by the burial detail. At the pit, the bodies were lined up side by side on the ground, while a chaplain held a graveside service. After the service the bodies were thrown into the pit. While the chaplain was offering a final prayer, one of the litter bearers thought he saw movement in the slimy mess and yelled. Someone else saw the same movement and quickly jumped into the mess, grabbed the arm of the young soldier, and pulled him up to the bank where others helped pull him out. He was put on one of the litters and hurried back to the hospital. Later, he liked to talk about his experiences and always finished by saying, "Maybe God can wait." This young man survived and was repatriated to the States. Apparently God did wait.

CHAPTER 11

About the middle of September, a large flight of planes crossed over Luzon, almost directly overhead. They were unfamiliar to us, but we knew that they were not Japanese planes because there were no Rising Sun insignias. They also didn't fly like the Japanese. The bombers flew in straight formation at considerable height, while fighters crisscrossed the area below the bombers. It was quite a sight. We watched as the planes few over in a westerly direction. A short time later, what appeared to be the same planes returned, flying easterly, and as they approached our position, one of the fighters made a low pass, directly over us, tipping his wings as he roared by, and climbed back into formation. This time there was no doubt whose planes they were. They were U.S. Navy planes!

Most of us were stunned. We wanted to shout and wave, but experience had taught us never to display our feelings. We didn't have long to wait, however. Those of us who were in camp were ordered into our barracks, and a work party that had been building an airfield for the Japanese about a mile away was quickly returned to camp.

The flights had become an almost daily ritual, and as the Japanese guards relaxed a little, we went on about our normal business. Morale began to soar because we felt that our forces were nearby now. It would be only a matter of time before we would finally be free.

Liberated prisoners pack meager possessions to leave (photo courtesy U.S. Navy).

A few days after the initial fly-over, a flight was returning from the west when we saw a Japanese bomber begin to take off from the nearby airfield. Out of the blue, one of the fighters roared low over the camp and rode that bomber almost like a piggy-back. Suddenly there was an explosion and the bomber disintegrated in a cloud of black smoke. Hallelujah!

The first week in October, the Japanese began to act like they did when a work detail was going to leave camp. There was a flurry of activity, including the usual inspections. This time, though, nearly everyone in camp was given a "physical" (a glass rod shoved up the rectum for a stool sample). I have no idea what the Japanese doctor did with the samples because everybody had dysentery. I think they were just interested in determining who could walk and who couldn't. I could now walk fairly well.

During the second week of October, two or three drafts of prisoners were transferred to Bilibid, and I was one of them. Until this time, we all talked about what we were to do when we got out. A few individuals had even entertained thoughts of not waiting for the Americans. They had elaborate plans for escape to greet the American troops before they got to camp. Our only hope now seemed to be the quick arrival of

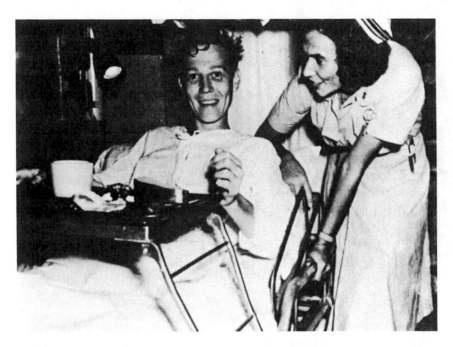

Happy with his first meal in a long time (photo courtesy U.S. Navy).

our troops. Why did it take them so long? We knew they were near. Unfortunately, all of the men who could have survived escape to meet the Americans were shipped out. Most of those who stayed had to be carried out by the Americans when they arrived there a few weeks later.

At Bilibid we found conditions much worse than before. The wards were filled with men in pitiful condition, their ribs showing under their tight skin, and their faces drawn from starvation. Most of them just sat or lay in a kind of quiet resignation of their fate. They talked little, even when the chaplains came around to talk with them. From mid–November to mid–December we did little but sit around, sometimes dreaming for the day of our release, sharing recipes or otherwise planning our return home. What would be the first thing we would do? The answer was always the same. Eat, eat, and eat some more. No one thought of anything else.

CHAPTER 12

On December 13, 1944, we finally left Bilibid, and were again marched through the streets of Manila to the dock area. This time, though, the streets were nearly empty. American planes had left their mark on the city. It was almost deserted except for a few Filipinos scurrying about. At the dock area the scene was one of total chaos. Sunk and damaged ships filled the bay almost as far as the eye could see. It seemed like one could almost walk across the bay on the hulks of ships.

The piers were in shambles. The buildings were almost totally destroyed. On closer look, channels had been cleared, allowing ships into and out of the dock area.

We had eaten early that day and had been given a ration to take with us, so the wait wasn't so bad, but most of us were still disappointed that the Americans had not reached us and liberated us as we had expected. The recent moratorium from the heavy bombing by the Americans made us a little wary that we might become a target at any time. It was a time of apprehension.

While Japanese women and children boarded the *Oryoku Maru*, a first class passenger liner, 1,619 prisoners stood waiting. Late in the afternoon, we boarded the ship while being checked off from a list held by the Japanese interpreter, Wada, and Lieutenant Toshino, the Japanese officer in charge.

The shambles that was Manila: February 12, 1945 (photo courtesy U.S. Navy).

As we boarded we were directed to a hold and herded between guards who prevented us from straying away from an invisible path. There were three holds, each about 30 feet wide by 50 feet long. Access to the holds was a hatch opening in the main deck about 12 feet square. The hatch opening was lined by a steel combing extending 2 or 3 feet above and below the main deck, which made the top unreachable to us without a ladder. As soon as a hold was loaded the ladders were removed.

According to records, there were 611 men crammed into the #1 hold, 189 in #2 hold, and 819 in #3 hold. I found myself in the #2 hold, located just forward of the bridge, which I could see from below. The uneven distribution of prisoners was the result of the Japanese taking too long to check names as we were boarding. The pace must have been too slow for the ship's crew, because there was a sudden order to "Speedo! Speedo." The Japanese pushed, shoved and flailed at the prisoners. They hustled us, tripping and falling most of the way, into the holds. Some of our officers protested the uneven distribution, but to no avail. Their complaints were met with rifle butts.

After the Japanese were satisfied that all of the prisoners were aboard, the ship got underway. Some tubs of steamed rice were lowered into the holds, along with tubs of cooked seaweed. Distribution was a problem at first, but that was soon solved by more rational heads, and everyone got their fair share. Shortly afterward, some metal 5-gallon cans containing water and tea were lowered into the holds, but darkness fell and prevented an even distribution.

The hold I was in was like a deep, dark dungeon. The others, we learned from later accounts, fared much worse. The crowding became a major problem almost immediately. The darkness, the lack of space, and especially the lack of air, caused panic in holds #1 and #3. The darkness and the close confinement made movement particularly difficult.

The holds were constructed so that the part directly under the main deck was bi-level. A shelflike platform provided only a 4-foot height on both levels. No one could stand up in the bays. Standing was only possible under the hatch opening and a part of that deck space had to be set aside for the benjo buckets (toilets). Congestion was so bad in our hold that it was difficult to get to the benjo buckets. Some used their canteens to urinate in. The canteens were then passed to the open area in the center, emptied and started on their way back again. Those who had to defecate were less fortunate. It was virtually impossible. With chronic diarrhea prevalent, the spaces farthest back became unlivable within hours. Words cannot explain the misery of those of us in hold #2, but it was much, much worse in the other two holds.

In the hold I was in, the heat, together with the salty seaweed supper, began its toll in terms of thirst, and the water and tea didn't last long. Some prisoners began to get noisy, and as the noise got louder, the Japanese threatened to close the hatch because we were disturbing the women and children. One guard pointed his rifle into the hold and threatened to shoot if we did not quiet down. The leaders in hold #2 were able to maintain some control, and the hatch cover was not closed. Those in the afterhold did not fare as well.

The #3 hold, with four times as many prisoners as the hold I was in, was located over the engine room, complicating the heat problem. In their case, the hatch opening was partially closed because of the noise, and many of those crowded back under the main deck were beginning to suffocate. Some attacked others to steal their canteens. There were several cases where an individual would go crazy and bite into the throat of another to get blood. Some drank urine, even though they were told that they would die a horrible death, and they did. Some individuals became so deranged that they had to be killed. It is amazing what dehydration can do to an individual. Equally amazing, though, was the indifference of the Japanese. They continued to ignore us until we became too noisy for them and then they threatened us. They acted less than human.

Despite terrible conditions, some people slept. It seemed incredible that, as crowded as we were, one could fall asleep. When a certain level of exhaustion was reached, sleep would come, even if one were standing up. In our case it was impossible to fall. Sometimes, when sleep came, the constant movement of the mass would result in the sleeper winding up on or near the deck. I often found myself in that predicament, and would start a struggle to reach an upright position again.

Suddenly, all hell broke loose! From my vantage point in the hold below, near the open hatch, I could see Japanese soldiers crawling up the ladders to reach the machine guns mounted above the bridge. Japanese were scurrying all over the main deck. Something was about to happen. I began to hear the noise of anti-aircraft fire, followed by the roar of dive bombers. I saw several soldiers knocked from those ladders as they tried to climb to the gun positions above, and some of the soldiers in the gun positions were thrown violently in the air. The strafing was accurate and deadly. There was no doubt that the attacking planes were American, and that there was no Japanese air opposition.

The bombing and strafing continued intermittently throughout the day. Some said there had been nine separate runs. To me, it seemed almost continuous. What puzzled some of us, though, was why we hadn't been sunk already. Most of us were resigned, by now, to going down with the ship.

The ferocity of the attack led many of us, at first, to believe that the Americans did not know we were on board. At any rate, we found ourselves cheering the planes on. Then when the attacks continued, we began to have a faint hope that maybe the Americans *did* know we were aboard. Otherwise, why would they not sink us outright? They certainly could have, because during the later runs there was no anti-aircraft fire from the *Oryoku Maru*. On one of the later runs a bomb hit the stern of the ship, almost directly over the afterhold, killing several and wounding many more. The bomb put a hole in the side of the ship, allowing air into the hold, and there was some relief from the suffocating conditions, but at a terrific price.

During one of the later runs, I was hit in the right upper back by a piece of shrapnel about 2 inches long, which I still carry around. The force of the blow took the wind out of me, and stunned me for a while. Because I was lodged in between the others, I couldn't fall. When the attacks were over, I was helped out of where I had been, and the man just behind me pitched forward, dead. It was obvious that the piece of shrapnel had gone through him before it struck me. I remember wondering whether or not I was lucky. If it had not gone through someone else, I would have been dead. A memory etched in my mind is that of watching an Army chaplain praying quietly on the deck, directly underneath the open hatch, as tracer bullets slammed into the wooden planking at his feet. To me, that act took more courage than I could ever imagine.

We learned later that there had been three other ships in our convoy, and that those ships had been loaded with Japanese troops. All of them had been sunk.

As darkness enveloped the ship for the second night, conditions were worse than the night before. More men were killed to keep them from killing others in their frenzy. Still more tried to kill themselves.

The bomb that hit the stern of the ship apparently damaged the steering mechanism and the ship could not get underway effectively. During the night, activity topside indicated that we were somewhere near shore, because the Japanese women and children topside were being evacuated.

This activity continued throughout the night. For us though, the miserable conditions prevented us from thinking clearly, and the anxiety of not knowing what was going on, was maddening. Were we going to be left where we were? Would the Americans return at daylight to finish the ship off? Should we try to get off the ship by ourselves? A careful look topside by a brave soul provided an answer. There were still guards topside manning machine guns.

We didn't have to wait long to find out what was going to happen to us. The Japanese officer in charge of the prisoners, Lt. Toshino, and his interpreter Sergeant Wada looked into the holds, and ordered that all wounded prisoners be brought topside for transfer to shore.

During the lull following the air attack on the ship, some of the doctors were called topside to treat the women and children. Working without food and water, they spent many hours helping the wounded, only to be shoved back into the holds later.

A substantial number of prisoners were doctors and chaplains, and it was a testament to those dedicated men that they continued to help, no matter how bad things were. A number of doctors died during this time, and those who were left worked even harder.

It was under the direction of the doctors and hospital corpsmen, that I was finally brought topside and led to the side of the ship were a lifeboat was tied. At the head of the ladder to the lifeboat stood Lt. Toshino and Wada. Wada was asking our names and Toshino was holding a list of prisoners on which he checked off our names.

When Wada said I could go, I was helped down into the lifeboat.

83

As I remember it, there were about a dozen of us in the small boat, and four Japanese were manning the oars.

As we pulled away, I recognized immediately where we were. We were in Subic Bay, just off the shore of Olongapo, about half-mile out. The thought crossed my mind that if I could get ashore, I could escape into the hills. As I daydreamed for a second, there was a loud explosion underneath the boat. I was suddenly thrown high into the air, looking down at what had been a boat. Pieces of the boat were passing me falling back down to the water. As soon as I hit the water, I looked around to orient myself. When I saw the seawall on the beach, I tore off my shirt and pants, keeping only my shoes tied around my neck. Then I headed for shore. My bad leg would not help me in swimming, and I felt some panic as I wondered if I could make it to shore. Alongside me, in the water, was another American, both of us swimming hard. Just as we got started, though, we felt the pressure of machine gun bullets landing near us. The sound was muffled, but there was no mistaking the feeling as the bullets hit near us. When I looked up, there was a dive bomber headed directly for us with tracer bullets looking like they were aimed at our heads. This time I rolled up in a ball and waited until the plane had made its run. Then I paddled for shore as fast as I could. Each time a plane made a run for us, I would repeat the process until I got ashore. Somehow, on the way in, I lost my shoes.

Both of us knew exactly where we were, and I think we both had the same idea. When the other man got his second wind he looked around to the ship to see what was happening. There was no activity that he could make out, so he went to the seawall, got a handhold in the rocks, and lifted himself up to see over the wall. As he stuck his head over the top, he was staring directly into a Japanese machine gun. "Look out!" he screamed, as he slid down to the beach. When he told me what he had seen, I had a sinking feeling in my gut. There was no chance of escape now!

As we sat on the beach with our backs to the seawall, we watched some of the men swimming toward the shore. As more of them headed for shore, there would be an occasional burst of machine gun fire over our heads. We found out later that the Japanese had set up their guns to keep the men from straying outside a certain line as they were coming ashore. Several men who could not swim never made it. Several swimmers helped the weak and injured. During the next few hours the men continued to swim from the ship. Some of them, when they got topside from the holds, discovered that there were no Japanese still aboard, and proceeded to go through the ship looking for food and water before machine gun bursts from the shore convinced them that they had better get ashore soon. Those who went through the ship reported that the damage was unbelievable. They also said that there were several dead Japanese crewman on the main deck.

There were still some men in the water, when a single U.S. Navy plane came in very fast from the east, sending the Japanese gunners to their shore guns. Before they could turn their guns around the plane had dropped a bomb on the *Oryoku Maru*. The ship seemed to explode midship and sank quickly. Some of our prisoners might have gone down with it. It lies there still, and every year there is a memorial at the site.

While the prisoners were being rounded up on the beach, the Japanese were quickly putting a fence around a cement surface that once had been a double tennis court in front of the old Marine barracks. During the next few hours, the survivors of the "Hell Ship" were herded into the fenced area. It was evening when the move was completed. We now had been without food or water for almost 48 hours. There was very little clothing and no cover. That night the cold was numbing, and there were several deaths. Deprivation of food and water, together with the drop in temperature, took its toll.

On the double tennis court, a portion was set aside as a "hospital." During the night, doctors worked feverishly to save the more seriously wounded men, but their efforts had little effect without needed medicines and supplies. The saddest thing was that there was no pain medication. The wounded had to take their pain "cold turkey." To some of them, death could be, and probably was, a relief from hell. In the morning, most of the wounded were dead.

CHAPTER 13

It is difficult to describe conditions on the morning of December 16. We had a meager supply of water, by way of a single water spigot. One half-inch water line for more than 1000 thirsty men. Men who had canteens quickly lined up to fill them, downed what they could, then got back in line to fill their canteens again. So far there was no sign of food.

First though, we had to get some organization. We needed to know how many men were still alive, and determine who was missing and presumed dead. To accomplish this, Lt. Toshino gave us his list of those starting the trip, and with the help of some senior military officers, a roll card was accomplished.

After past experience on Corregidor, at Bilibid, and at Cabanatuan, and now this tragic experience, I firmly believed that our continued survival would depend on the leadership of our officers, and the ability of the enlisted men to organize under that leadership. In the beginning, the Japanese had attempted to drive a wedge between the officers and enlisted men hoping to "divide and conquer." The officers successfully argued with the Japanese, that it would be in the best interest of the Japanese themselves to allow the Americans to have some military discipline among ourselves. To that end, we succeeded, and many lives were saved that might not otherwise have been.

It was reported that there were 1340 surviving prisoners from the *Oryoku Maru*, including 200 wounded. Of the 1619 men who left Manila on December 13, 279 men died, some by suicide, some killed when they attacked others in their frenzy to get relief from thirst, but most because of the poor conditions and treatment.

The next task was to find space enough for 1140 men to lie down. The space available, after an area had been set aside for a hospital, was about 60 feet by 80 feet. In his book, *Captured on Corregidor*, Army Lieutenant, (now retired Lt. Gen.) John M. Wright, Jr., describes how the men were arranged in ranks across the width of the double tennis court in such a way as to make the best use of space for sleep. The spacing resulted in about 15 inches between men, so that no one could lie on his back. In order to turn from side to side, every man in the row had to turn at the same time. This was very difficult, because when someone wanted to turn over, somebody had to be awakened before they could turn. This interlocking scheme was no doubt devised by competent minds. I could not have imagined a better utilization of space. At least we could lie down, which we could not do any other way. For some it was the first chance to lie down, with at least a little comfort, since Manila.

On this same day, December 16, American dive bombers came back again and demonstrated their skills by blowing up a fuel depot quite near our position. They also destroyed a dock area used by the Japanese. I remember watching those dive bombers making slow, deliberate runs through the thick anti-aircraft fire put up by the Japanese. A natural instinct would have been to hit the ground, but everybody stood up and watched in awe, as those pilots went about their work. The targets were so close that some of the debris from the explosions landed in our space. I was confident that the Americans were close enough now to save us from further misery. How wrong I was.

After three more days without food, the Japanese gave us one bag of uncooked rice for the entire group. To be fair, the officers divided the men into groups. The group leader would draw the ration for his group, which he divided among the men, Then, after each group had their share if there was any rice left, it was given to one group to divide, on a rotating basis, until the rice was gone. On the next serving, the rice was divided among the groups with any surplus given to the next group on the list. There was no fairer way to distribute the meager rations. To make the ration of raw rice seem like more than it was, some of the men soaked the grains in water (if they could get water). I could not wait that long, but I did chew the grains slowly so that the grains seemed to last longer.

For the next few days, the regimen was about the same, except that on one of those days we were allowed out to lounge on a grassy area nearby. It was a great feeling. But that little sojourn ended when the guards started yelling, "Speedo! Speedo," and we were herded back into our area.

On December 20, our hopes were raised a little when the Japanese told us that some of us would be leaving that day. I was one who felt that, after what had happened, there was no way that the Japanese could ever get us out of the Philippines so we were probably going back to Manila.

At noon, about half of the men were loaded into trucks, packed almost as closely as they had been on the tennis court. They took a bag of raw rice with them. As yet there was no word about where they were going. After the prisoners departed, the rest of us were told to be ready to leave the following day.

On the next day we were loaded into trucks, as those who left the day before had been, with our bag of raw rice. We took off, winding through the jungle roads until we cleared the jungle, then raced across the open until we reached San Fernando, Pampango. Those who had left the day before had been billeted in the provincial jail for security. The rest of us were kept in the town theater, which had a lot of room in comparison with where we had been previously. That evening we got some cooked rice. It was a real treat.

San Fernando was a rail center, previously providing service from Manila to various parts of Bataan and points north. Its main tracks bordered Clark Field on the south. Clark Field was a major Army Air Corps base in the Orient before the war, and was now being used by the Japanese for their fighters and bombers.

During the next 24 hours in San Fernando there were at least two American air attacks on Clark Field. It seemed that wherever the Japanese put us, there would be American fighters and bombers on the attack as if to welcome us. The more of this activity I saw, the more convinced I was that the Japanese would be unable to get us out now.

On December 23, we were given enough food to fill our stomachs for the first time. This led me to think that I was right. The Japanese would be fattening us up for the turnover. We still thought we would be returning to Manila, when Lt. Toshino asked for a list of prisoners who were too sick to walk. We assumed that they would be taken to Manila. Given the names by our doctors, Lt. Toshino and his guards led the men away. I learned that Lt. Toshino had taken these very sick men to the local cemetery where he supervised their execution, over a mass grave.

Early in the morning of the 24th, we were ordered into formation and marched to the railroad station where a line of freight cars waited for us. The engineer had the steam up and was ready to go. The cars we were to board were considerably smaller than ones in the United States, and the tracks were narrow guage. The system reminded me of a large model railroad. The cars measured about 7 feet wide and about 40 feet long with an interior height of about 6 feet. At 5 feet 11½ inches, my head just cleared the top. With almost 200 men stuffed into each tiny car, we had less room than in the *Oryoku Maru*, if that were possible. There was only one 6-foot-wide door in each car, and four guards stood in this space to make sure nobody escaped. A heavy rope across the open door held everyone in. Some of the prisoners had been placed on top of the cars with instructions to wave at American planes, if they should attack, and attack they did.

As our train passed the eastern boundary of Clark Field we could see Japanese planes in camouflaged bunkers. Just then attacking U.S. Navy planes came in low over our train to attack those planes on the ground. Fortunately, the men on top did their job, and we were spared annihilation.

I remember the train making a couple of stops on the way north. During those stops, some of the men were allowed to get off briefly to stretch a little. During the trip a few men had passed out from the heat and lack of air, despite the open door, and during the stops a special effort was made to get these men off the cars into open air, even if it were only for a few minutes. As soon as they were revived a little, they were put back on the car to continue the trip. As the cars were pulling away, several Filipinos rushed to the open door, dodging the guards' rifle butts, and handed some fruit to those in front of the door. This miserable trip lasted for 19 hours.

We arrived in San Fernando on Christmas Eve, 1944. Those of us without shoes found the forced march through the town on crushed coral roads very painful. Eventually we came to a school building, with a fenced yard, where we were assembled and accounted for.

The next day was Christmas and we received two meals of rice and comotes (sweet potatoes). Water was, however, a problem again. There was no supply at the school, so some men were allowed to get water from a nearby source. It was obvious that the water they brought back was grossly contaminated. The Japanese had given us some medical supplies, however, and among the supplies was some iodine which was added to the water. It wasn't appetizing but it was water. Also included in the medical supplies were some sulfathiazole and quinine (for malaria). It began to look like we would be here for some time, so our officers began to organize us into groups for rationing food and water, as we had been doing since we left Bilibid almost two weeks ago.

At this point I had a pair of khaki pants and a shirt, but I can't remember where I got them. I was no worse off than most, and better off than some. I froze at night and roasted in the sun during the day.

Just before dark on Christmas day, we got the order to assemble in four columns four abreast, and we hit the road again. After about two miles we came upon the beach at Lingayan Bay. (This was where the Japanese had made their initial landings when they attacked the Philippines in December of 1941.) We were ordered to stay in formation of fours, but we could lie down and rest.

While we were waiting, a large truck arrived with rations in the form of gooey rice balls, which were good. Any food was good. Water was still a problem and we did the same thing as at the school, only we had no iodine now. A detail was sent to get water, and they came back with buckets, cans and bottles of water that was as foul as that at the school, but we had nothing to sanitize it with. It probably didn't matter: we all had dysentery anyway.

After we had eaten we were marched down to the beach, through Japanese gun positions, pill boxes, and fox holes. Some of us were directed to get into a foxhole and stay there with the Japanese riflemen. It was obvious that they were expecting an American landing momentarily. What a situation to be in. I never understood the rationale of that move. It began to seem as if the Japanese were deliberately moving us around, just to be targets for the Americans.

A few men at a time were allowed to go into the bay to bathe. I declined. At this point I estimated that I weighed less than 90 pounds. I was tired. My bones ached and there were pressure sores on my elbows and hips. It was painful just to lie down. I didn't know how anybody had made it this far. There was so little water and food. I think that some of us were surviving out of stubbornness. Every day a few men died. I remember that, on occasions, I envied those who had died; their suffering was over, their journey ended. How much more would we have to suffer before we could join them? The answer came sooner than expected!

CHAPTER 14

That night we marched again. We ended up on a pier in Lingayan Bay. The bay held several Japanese freighters and there were a number of other ships that had made their final voyage. Lying in shallow water, those hulks stood out in start contrast to the low tide.

Two of the freighters were troop transports. The bay was very busy with landing barges, bringing troops and ammunition and guns to shore, then swinging over toward our pier to pick us up to take us out to the transports. Nearly 900 men had been ferried to one of the transports, the *Enoura Maru*, as I waited my turn. Then, suddenly activity was speeded up and the rest of us, more than 200, were rushed to a second transport, the *Brazil Maru*.

During the transfer of men from the pier to the landing barges, there were a few accidents because of a drop of about 20 feet from the pier to the barge where there was no ladder. There were several broken bones and assorted injuries. One man fell, striking his head on the rail of the barge and was dead when pulled from the water. He was left on the beach. As usual, there was no treatment for the injuries. To this day, I can't understand how some who sustained serious injuries, without treatment, continued to live.

The *Brazil Maru* was much better than the *Oryoku Maru* in terms of space for us. Our hold was two decks below the main deck, which was inhabited by wounded Japanese soldiers who were being transferred back to Japan.

Our deck space was more than adequate, but it was very cold, since the hatch was open with no cover. We had the customary 5-gallon cans for sanitary facilities, but there was still a shortage of water. We did get some rice daily, though, so we felt that we were faring better.

That night it was much more comfortable because we were not packed as we had been on the first ship. We could lie down, and for warmth two or three would get close together to share body heat.

We had not been underway long when I noticed that the skip kept turning, as if it were following the shore line of Luzon Island on its way north. The maneuvering probably was an effort to avoid American submarines. During most of the night, the ship would turn, then stop, then turn again. As daylight approached, we seemed to pick up speed, as if making a dash across some open water. Having been on our own submarines, I could appreciate what the skipper of this ship was going through. I didn't really care how he felt, because if one of our submarines spotted this ship, we would all die.

As expected, we did not go unnoticed. In the morning hours, the quiet was broken as Japanese sailors manned the deck guns. After a few rounds of fire, there would be a moment of silence, followed by yelling and applause, as the torpedo missed. We came under attack several times during the next few days, always signalled by frantic activity topside, followed by the hearty cheer, "Bonzai! Bonzai!' when the attack was over. This activity continued for three days, with periods of time spent in dropping depth charges for 20 or 30 minutes at a time. We could feel the depth charges and my mind went back to my days on submarines before the war.

After three days and nights we finally arrived in Takao Harbor, Formosa. It was cold and miserable, and we were really hungry. Our miseries had not stopped, nor did our hunger and thirst. Several more men died on this last trip. It was New Year's Day, 1945. Our count was now down to about 1300 from 1619 men who started the trip on December 13, 1944.

The conditions on the *Oryoku Maru* were replicated on the *Brazil Maru*, only much more so, as we sat in the harbor. What started out to be a relatively good trip went bad as we lay at anchor. Again, some of the men became unruly, even combative. The combined lack of food, water, and rest, made everybody edgy and less tolerant. Who was to blame them? Coupled with uncontrollably filthy conditions, we were just about at the animal stage. This amused the Japanese, and they seemed to delight in seeing us behave like animals.

When both transports had reached Takao, the men from the *Brazil Maru* were moved to the *Enoura Maru* with about half of them (about 300) placed in the hold just below where I was, just forward of the bridge. The other half were moved into the afterhold.

After a couple of days, the men who had just been put in the hold below us were brought up and moved into the hold just forward of us, near the bow of the ship, on our same level. Most of those men moved to the forward hold were medics, and I had thought of joining them, but somehow I did not have the strength to make the move, even if I could have gotten away with it. The hold below us had been filled with partially refined sugar.

On the morning of January 9, the sound of anti-aircraft fire interrupted our rice rationing. United States Navy planes were making a run on us, and before we had a chance to seek cover, the first dive-bomber scored a direct hit on the forward hold, killing nearly everyone in the hold. After the attack was over, the Japanese refused to go into either hold to help, so it was some time before anyone knew the extent of the damage.

In the hold I was in the hatch covers were smashed, and the heavy planks were falling down on the deck below, forcing everybody to crawl as far back in the hold as possible. Some of those who were next to the external bulkheads were injured by shrapnel from the armor-piercing bullets as they opened up the side of the ship.

Those who could, helped others away from the debris. Some of the men, late to seek cover away from the hatch opening, turned their backs to the opening, rather than face what was happening underneath the hatch. Some of them picked splinters of wood or steel from their backs for some time afterward. I was not hurt, although most of those around me appeared dead.

Sometime after the attack was over, the Japanese did allow our medics to go into the forward hold, but they themselves refused to go in. I couldn't go, but those who did said that I should be glad that I hadn't gone. One doctor said that there might be a few men, at the most, who were alive. The tragic thing about it was that nothing could be done for them.

The number of injuries and deaths in this one attack probably outnumbered the casualties we had already had since the start of the trip. There were probably 300 men killed in the forward hold alone, and I don't know how many were dead in the hold I was in. I could only guess at the body count as they piled up under the open hatch. To make matters worse, the Japanese refused to allow the bodies to be removed.

For the next three or four days, it was generally quiet in the hold.

It was extremely cold, so cold that I was crawling around the deck to find a warm body to lie next to, then falling asleep, only to wake up cold, and finding the man next to me was dead.

Sometimes three or four of us would huddle together, then change positions frequently, so that we all shared in the warmth as well as the cold.

The rations continued to be about the same, half a cup of rice once or twice a day, sometimes with a little vegetable ingredient, more often without. During the lull following the bombing, someone found their way into the hold just below where I was, where the sugar had been loaded. Sugar began to show up among the prisoners. For some reason, I failed to get some, so I watched carefully and found out how it was being done and followed suit. I found that I could squeeze myself through the opening between the edge of the deck and the side of the ship, a space of about 8 inches wide. I had no difficulty getting down, and I sent a lot of sugar upward, but when I felt that I had been down long enough (and out of fear that I would be caught), I had a problem trying to get back through the same opening. I found that I didn't have the strength to pull myself back up, and I began to panic. After pushing several sacks of sugar to the side where I was going up, I managed to get my head and arms through the small space, and was pulled the rest of the way by a couple of stronger men. I was so scared that I shook for an hour. It wasn't long before the Japanese discovered that sugar was being pilfered from the lower hold, and they demanded that the culprits be turned over to them. Immediately I became a devout coward. I had a good idea what would happen if I volunteered, and the more I thought about it, the more scared I became. Then word came down to us that no more rice would be issued until the guilty men came up topside. I still held out, hoping that someone else would be brave enough to confess. I certainly wasn't the only one down there. Within hours two men volunteered to go topside. I don't know who the men were, but I had a healthy respect for their bravery. I have never really forgotten that episode, nor have I forgotten how I failed the test of bravery. I was not proud of my actions. I was very glad to learn that the two men who did surrender to the Japanese received only light punishment and were returned to the hold.

During this time there were more deaths and the Japanese still refused to allow us to take the bodies topside. The smell became almost intolerable. When there were about 40 or more bodies, the Japanese sent down a sling on which the bodies were loaded. The bodies were then hoisted to the main deck, and from there to a lighter alongside the ship. From there, I understand, some bodies were taken to a cemetery and buried in a mass grave. Others were piled up on the beach and burned. The men who volunteered for this work got no extra rations and no extra water. They did a heroic job under the circumstances.

On January 14, those prisoners who had survived on the *Enoura Maru* were transferred to the *Brazil Maru*. Several men died while being transported and were carried along as the rest of us boarded the ship. Within three or four days of getting underway, prisoners were dying at the rate of 10 or 20 per day, with burial over the side in a dirty yellow sea. There were no ceremonies and no prayers. I felt that maybe we were beyond prayer. As soon as the men died, their clothes were stripped of valuables, if any, and were taken by the first one to find the person dead. The clothes were set aside in one corner and given to anybody who needed them. Most of the clothing was caked with feces, and there was no way to launder them. The hold I was in had been occupied by horses, and some manure was still piled up in the center of the deck when we arrived. We cleaned it up as soon as the Japanese would let us. We were able to crawl into the bays underneath the hatch opening, even though it was terribly crowded. After the center part of the deck space was cleared, it became a sick bay for the sickest men to be cared for by the medics who could still help.

After five or six days the death toll reached as many as 30 per day. By this time, the only source of water was evaporation from the ship's boilers. It was brackish and difficult to drink, even as thirsty as we were!

Sanitary facilities on the *Brazil Maru* were better, in that the latrine was attached to the outside rail of the ship, and extended out over the water. The heavy seas made using the latrine an unpleasant experience, since we were usually doused with salt water when the ship rolled.

On January 28, 1945, we arrived at Moji, on Kyushu Island, Japan. For the last few days the Japanese would not allow us to dump the dead bodies in the ocean, so the bodies were stacked on the deck under the hatch opening, and the stack had reached a height of over 5 feet by the time we tied up at the dock.

After more than six weeks of starvation, dehydration, beri beri, pellagra, scurvy, and finally pneumonia from exposure to the extreme cold, not to mention diseases from contaminated food and water, it is a wonder that there were any survivors at all. There were no medications for any of the illnesses, and there was no relief from recontamination. We had just completed a voyage of unspeakable hell, and we were not yet through. Of 1619 prisoners who left Manila on December 13, 1944, less than 500 half-dead souls arrived at Moji, Japan. Many of those survivors would still die.

A Japanese medical detail came aboard, took one look at us, and appeared shocked at what they saw. They would not go into the hold, instead we had to climb out of the hold and submit to another physical examination, including the glass rod test. A quick look at our throats, and a pretense at listening to our chests, sufficed for a physical examination while we stood naked on the main deck. At least one man died during this fiasco. When the exams were over we were issued some Japanese clothing, consisting of a pair of woolen underwear, a warm shirt, wool pants and shoes (there was no choice as to fit). The temperature that day was about 20°F.

When the Japanese had finished their show, we were marched a few blocks through the snow to an open air theater where we found a water tap. Water! It was almost unbelievable. But the tap was frozen with barely a trickle of water. Someone discovered some barrels of water, which were intended for fire fighting, however, and some proceeded to gorge themselves. The doctors had warned everybody about this cold water, that it should be taken slowly, until the body acclimated itself. A few men heeded their advice, and I'm glad that I was one of them. Sure enough, some of the men began to cry out in agony, as the extremely cold water doubled them over with cramps. Two or three men died during that day, but I'm sure that the water was not the only cause. They were already very ill and weak before the cold water episode.

At this point, the men were divided into four groups for transfer to various prison camps. Group I went to Camp 3. Group II was sent to Camp 1, and group III was sent to Camp 17, all on Kyushu Island. About 120 of us were determined to be unable to make it to the regular camps, and were sent to what appeared to be a military hospital, a low frame building with no heat. There, we were given a straw mat and plenty of blankets. Under those blankets I started to get warm for the first time in many weeks. It is difficult to put into words the luxurious feeling of warmth, after being so cold for so long.

It didn't take long to learn that very few buildings in Japan had central heat. The buildings were constructed in long straight rows, so that a single steam pipe running through one room in each building would provide a minimum source of heat. The steam usually originated from an electrical generating plant.

Soon after we were settled in, we were issued a small box containing some rice and salty fish. For the first time in a long time, I was comfortable and not hungry. I must have slept for a long time, for it was daylight when I awakened. Even though I slept the sleep of exhaustion, I was being tormented with head lice, body lice, and fleas.

A Japanese medic came on the ward carrying a 5-gallon intravenous (IV) bottle. It was apparently filled with an IV fluid. I suspect it was the standard treatment for dehydration, a mixture of dextrose (sugar) in normal saline (0.9 percent salt).

He took two lengths of IV tubing in his hands and he hooked up a "Y" connection to each of the pieces, so that he had four separate lines coming from the bottle of IV fluid. He then put an IV needle on the end of each line. After putting a needle into a vein in one arm of each of four men, lying in a row, the medic allowed the fluid to run for awhile. He then removed the needles from the first four men, and put them in the next four men. It appeared to me that he did not change the needles between patients.

In a few days I was running a fever, as were several others. I first thought it might be the IV treatment. After deliberation with the Japanese doctor, those of us with fevers were moved into another ward for isolation. The diagnosis was diphtheria.

It was during this isolation that a Japanese officer informed us that we should say a prayer for our president, who had just died. That is how we were informed of the death of President Franklin Delano Roosevelt. I believe that the Japanese had some respect for him, even though we were at war.

On another occasion, a Japanese doctor came on the ward, and asked, through an interpreter, if any of us could understand German. No one volunteered, so he spoke in Japanese, using an interpreter. He told us that this area of Japan was expecting air attacks by American planes (B-29s), in retaliation for some Japanese bombing attacks on New York City. He gave us specific instructions to the effect that if anyone left the building during an air raid, they would be "shot killed." As we later learned, it was unusual for the Japanese to stay inside during an air raid, but we could stay inside—we were expendable.

After a few days in isolation, I was returned to the general ward. By the time I was out of isolation, I was able to get around fairly well. With another hospital corpsman I helped distribute the few medications the Japanese made available. It helped to have something to do.

From over 100 men who came to this hospital, there were only about 30 still alive. The physical and mental assault they had suffered, without any foreseeable end to their suffering, was more than some could handle. They had lost hope. For me, I was not ready to give up without a fight.

On February 24, a detail was assembled under Captain Wermuth (the one-man army of Bataan) for transfer to another camp. I was included in that draft, having just been released from isolation. We traveled by ambulance to the train station. I remember that on the train the window blinds were drawn, to prevent us from seeing the countryside (or was it to keep the Japanese civilians from seeing us?). Most likely it was because of the continuous American air threat. This procedure was common practice where we were concerned. Everytime we traveled anywhere by road or rail, we were hidden from view as much as possible.

The new facility was Camp 22, Fukuoka, Japan. When we arrived at this camp, we were greeted warmly by nearly 100 Australians, who had been captured in Singapore. They opened their Red Cross boxes and their hearts to us. We all looked so bad that the Australians did everything possible to help us get back on our feet. There were a few Dutch prisoners who had been taken in Indonesia. They ignored us. I got the feeling that they didn't care much for Americans. One of the things, besides the food, that gave us a great morale boost, was our first bath in more than three months. It was also the first hot bath since the war started, almost three years before. The bath was typical of the kind the Japanese still use.

The Japanese called it *atsui* (pronounced hotsee). It consisted of a heated pool, about 10 feet square, with a depth of about 4 feet. There was an adequate, but unheated, shower to prewash before entering the pool. The Australians helped us in the shower as well as in the pool, including help with our clothing. We were issued some ragged but serviceable cotton clothing which the Australians proceeded to wash for us. It seemed like a new world. We were very sick and very tired. I'm sure that nothing else would have been more appreciated than what had been done for us.

In stark contrast to the attitude of the Australians, was the attitude of the Dutch, especially the Dutch doctor. He was a native of one of the Dutch colonies, and was trained as a gynecologist. He appeared to have little knowledge of anything else in medicine. He also seemed to have a disgust for Americans. He ignored us, as well as our needs. It wasn't until later when a couple of our Navy doctors arrived in our camp that our medical needs were addressed to the extent possible.

With a little better diet, augmented by the Red Cross boxes, it didn't take long to get back on my feet. I was then able to work on the ward, giving medications, as well as washing bandages for reuse. In time I was playing chess with the Japanese medic, who was able to get some medications for us.

One night, while I was playing chess with the Japanese medic, in his pharmacy, two guards appeared in the doorway, pointed at me, and said something in Japanese, which I did not understand. I quickly stood up and bowed to the guards. One of them pointed his bayonet at my middle and made a motion to the outside, indicating that I should go with him. I did not argue; I went. It was obvious both guards meant business.

I can remember trying to think what it was that I might have done to deserve punishment, and I didn't even know what the punishment was going to be. I began to panic. I had seen this happen to others, and knowing what happened to them, made me think the worst. The guards led me to the outside of the building to the guardhouse at the main gate. At the gate, I was ordered to sit on the ground in front of the guards. Once on the ground, a pan of water was placed in front of me, and I was directed to put my hands in the water and keep them there. From 10 PM until the next morning, my hands never came out of the freezing water. Yet, despite the snow on the ground, and the low air temperature, my hands did not freeze. What saved my hands was probably that I kept moving them as much as I could without being obvious.

The episode that night was explained later by one of the officers in the group. It seems that someone had broken into the kitchen and stolen a large amount of food that was intended for the sickest patients in the hospital. The man accused was the lone survivor of a Japanese prison ship sunk enroute to Japan from the Philippines. He was an Army medic and the only American at Camp 22 when we arrived a few days earlier. It was understandable that he would talk to me, as we did have something in common. According to reports of the incident, the man was caught and accused, but would not or could not reveal the location of the stolen food. The Japanese asked Rogers who his friend was (I assume they figured that he had given the stolen food to a friend) and he gave them my name. The end result was that I suffered innocently.

Another incident, at about the same time, was rewarding rather than punitive. It involved a Japanese guard. The guard had fallen while repairing the guardhouse roof. In the fall, he had suffered a 2-inch laceration on his scalp. He came into the dispensary for care, and there was no one there but me. He spoke enough English that I was able to talk to him. I explained to him that I thought he would need sutures. The Japanese medic came in and, after talking to the guard, asked me if I could do a suture job. I lied and said I was not trained to do that kind of work. Apparently the Japanese medic was not trained either.

Eventually, after explaining the procedure to the Japanese medic, I wound up shaving the area and applying a "butterfly" adhesive bridge to close the laceration. The guard seemed happy with the job, and his wife brought some cookies to me on a couple of occasions. This was the first time I remember feeling treated humanely by any Japanese.

During the last week in April, we were informed that we were going to be moved again. As before, the news was not received enthusiastically. It had been our experience that most of the moves we had made were not for the better.

CHAPTER 15

One morning we boarded trucks (with the usual high sides), and proceeded to Fukuoka, a shipping port. There we were led to a space on the dock area near some freighters (not the safest place to be). During the evening hours, there were air raid alarms that delayed our boarding until morning. It was strange but few of us were afraid any more.

The following morning, we boarded a trim, clean boat, that was probably a ferry. The prisoners were allowed to sit or lie down on the deck in the large passenger space, while Japanese civilians, who boarded at the same time, occupied the more comfortable seating area. We had been issued a rice ration the day before, so it was quite a surprise when we were issued about a third of a cup of steamed rice.

In the late afternoon we arrived at a port facility which we were told was Fusan (Pusan), Korea. From the port facility we were marched (I was helped) the short distance to a large theater building which was located near a railroad terminal. All of the prisoners who made the trip from Fukuoka were survivors of the *Oryoku Maru*. They came from the four different camps on Fukuoka Island, so we had a chance to see old friends again, and share experiences.

Always, when we traveled, the prisoners were divided into groups with an American officer in charge under the direct supervision of the Japanese guards. This was done for security and accountability.

There was a good meal of steamed rice, seaweed and dried fish, and water was available. It was early evening and we were visiting with friends when our guards called for us to assemble. The flurry of activity was a surprise to us because we had just been told that we would all be leaving in the morning. Whenever something like this happened, the anxiety level always increased, and this spawned rumors. We were told that those leaving that night would be traveling for a day, and the rest of us would be traveling for two days. Speculation by some of the American officers would have the first group going to some place in Korea, and the rest to Manchukuo (Manchuria).

Those being shipped out were given a meal of rice and seaweed. They boarded one of the trains nearby, leaving in a northerly direction. I have no idea where they went.

That night in the theater passed rather quickly, and we were fairly comfortable, except for the anxiety about our destination. We were awakened early and given our rations, then ordered aboard another train ready at the depot. When everybody was aboard, we headed north. The cars we boarded were passenger coaches with upholstered seats. They had all the comforts of our trains back home (1920 vintage). In fact, a metal plate over one of the windows was stamped, "Made in Cincinnati, Ohio." On second look, the comfort factor evaporated as four men were assigned to a double seat, but being able to walk around, and sleeping in shifts made conditions a little better. I avoided the discomfort by getting some friends to help me up on the luggage rack above the seats. I was comfortable, and I was able to stay there most of the trip.

During the first day, we made two stops and were rewarded with good meals of steamed rice and seaweed with some dried fish. There was also an adequate amount of water available.

As before, we were ordered not to lift the window curtains, or we would risk punishment. Several of those nearest the windows were able to cheat a little and gave us a running account of the scenery which they reported was hilly and beautiful. Apparently the fruit trees were in bloom. Traveling on through the night we were told that the terrain was getting mountainous.

The second day the terrain was still mountainous and winding, but not as pretty as the day before. At one of the stops on the second day, the meals we had been given were sent back as unacceptable by the Japanese doctor who was traveling with us, and it was two hours before we got more. We were not used to this protective action by the Japanese, so some were upset. I believe that the Japanese doctor was the same one who was in charge of the hospital at the camp where we were going. He seemed to be unusually kind.

Sometime during the second night, we stopped in a city which we were told was Mukden, Manchukuo (Manchuria). After a few hours we moved a few miles to Camp Hoten, our destination.

The camp was located just a few miles outside the city of Mukden, the capital of Manchukuo. The area was agriculturally and industrially similar to the American Midwest. There was a number of small factories in the area, and most of the prisoners worked in these factories. Small arms, ammunition, tools and leather were some of the industries which used prisoner labor.

The buildings were two-story frame barracks. They were unheated, except for a wood stove on the first floor which was used for a couple of hours on the coldest evenings. Space was adequate, and mats of straw-like material were used for sleeping. We had blankets and enough clothing for comfort. I was glad that we had arrived at this camp late in the spring, because we had been told that the temperature in mid-winter had reached 35 degrees below zero.

The diet was adequate, but different. The first food we had was a big surprise for me. For the first time since imprisonment we had real wheat flour and corn meal in the form of biscuits or muffins. There was a variety of vegetables on the menu, although still not in quantities sufficient to maintain good health.

On arrival in camp, my group (mostly medical personnel and a few chaplains) were kept separate from the main camp for a few days until it was determined that we were not a medical threat to the "old-timers," most of whom had been there since 1942. Despite the separation, some of the men in the main camp managed to get to our side with offerings from their Red Cross packages. Some even managed to bring hot water to us in 5-gallon buckets.

As soon as we moved into the main camp, most of the American prisoners did everything they could for us, in addition to their working at their factory jobs. In direct contrast to the Americans, about 100 English and perhaps a dozen Dutch officer prisoners ignored us completely. They did not work, and all of them had sideboys (enlisted personal servants, who were themselves prisoners). In all my contacts with the English and Dutch, I found them to be distant and very arrogant. They all looked wealthy and in much better shape than we were. To them we probably looked terrible, and we did.

When we moved into the main compound, I was put in the hospital as a patient. It was still difficult for me to walk. Many of the incoming prisoners had difficulty coping with the food we were getting, because our systems couldn't tolerate the roughage. The usual symptoms were gastric distress, and some diarrhea, usually relieved as tolerance to the food increased. We were to learn more about this when we returned home.

Mine was a different problem. I had apparently picked up a Giardia infection, which caused an intestinal impaction. I was absolutely miserable until Navy Commander Carey Smith removed the impaction. Then I could cope.

The first or second day in the hospital, the Japanese made the large heated pool available to us, and with help from some of the stronger men, we were able to bathe and use the pool. It is difficult to describe how good a hot bath can be, when one is in the condition we were in. The hot bath in Japan had been our first, so we already knew how good it felt.

When I was returned to my bed after my visit to the pool, I found my Red Cross box gone, along with what few possessions I had managed to hang onto, including the food that I had traded cigarettes for. There was nothing I could do but report it to the Japanese, who responded immediately.

A Japanese officer appeared on the hospital ward to respond to the report of the theft, and while everybody stood (or sat) at attention, he proceeded to inspect every bunk and space. When he got to me, he turned the pillow aside and found the little metal first-aid kit that I used for cigarette butts. There was not a word spoken. The officer stood up in front of me and looked at me. It suddenly seemed as if the lights went out. He had hit me with a backhand that knocked me to the floor. I had never been hit so hard. The Japanese were deathly afraid of fire, and there was evidence that I had broken the rule against smoking in the building. No trace of the missing Red Cross box was ever found.

As my condition improved, I started to walk better, and before long I was doing well enough to leave the hospital and move to the regular barracks. From then on, I was able to do my own laundry and take care of myself. Sometime in June, I developed a toothache and sought out Navy dentist Fraleigh, who had been the dentist on the *Canopus* prior to the war. He took a look at the molar and diagnosed the problem as an abscess. The only treatment, he told me, was extraction. He also told me that he didn't have the necessary tools, but that he could pull it. If the tooth were not pulled, he said, there was a good chance that the infection would spread to my system, and in my condition, that would be bad news. The pain was so bad that I would have agreed to almost anything. There was no anesthesia. I said, "OK, let's go." He put me in a straight-backed chair and, while the Japanese doctor held my head down on the back of the chair, Doctor Fraleigh reached in with a pair of pliers, and pulled that molar as efficiently as any I had ever had pulled. The relief was instantaneous.

After that experience, I learned from Dr. Fraleigh that there were practically no dental caries (cavities) during our years in prison, probably because of little or no sugar in our diets. My problem was not caries, but an infection from poor dental care. When I got out of prison camp, I had only one cavity. I did have several loose teeth that eventually required extraction and some bridge work. Those of us who had only loose teeth to worry about were indeed lucky. Some of the men had had their teeth ground down to the gum line with a triangular file, as a means of torture. The Japanese would file in between the teeth to the gum line, leaving a line of jagged points. I still shudder at the thought of something like that happening.

As I mentioned before, most of the enlisted men and most of the American officers worked in various factories that were located in the area of the camp. The routine for the workday called for the prisoners to muster with their respective shooting squads just inside the main gate. Then, when a group was ready, the assigned guards would lead them through the gate, while the gate guards inspected the prisoners' lunch boxes. The actual inspection was cursory and the prisoners would be waved on through without delay. After a few months of that routine, the process became boring to the guards, and a prisoner could carry almost anything through without detection, both in and out of camp.

One day in June 1944 a young Marine private, who had been in my unit on Corregidor, took advantage of the laxity in the check-through system. On that particular evening, Billy Joe appeared late for his group. All of the groups had been checked through and were well on their way. When he rushed up to the gate, he held his open box for the guard to see. Then, still in a mock hurry, he raced off toward the factory where he was to go to work. When he was out of sight of the gate guard, he disappeared. Apparently he wasn't missed for several hours. It wasn't until late that evening that the soldiers brought Billy Joe back through the gate. Death was his punishment for trying to escape. That incident didn't surprise me as much as it did the Japanese, because I knew the man quite well. Under the most severe pressure, he was always one of the coolest individuals I ever knew. His behavior under fire was always a good example for me. His escape attempt worried some of his "shooting squad" more than a little, but nothing else happened.

At this point, most of the men in the medical group I was in had adjusted fairly well. The food was not too bad, although there was still

105

a lack of protein. Our Red Cross boxes helped a little, but we still needed protein.

Air raid activity over the area was increasing and the Japanese had the stronger men building air raid shelters in a fever of activity.

We all anticipated air raids and looked forward to them as an indication that the end of the war was getting close. Our big concern was that the end might not be soon enough. We had heard so many stories concerning the weather in this area that we dreaded the possibility of spending a winter here.

CHAPTER 16

On August 14, 1945, someone spotted some brightly colored parachutes dropping from the sky. Our immediate thought was that the Russians were attacking Mukden by air and it wouldn't be long now. There were both tears and cheers, but the cheers were dampened because we didn't want to upset the Japanese guards while they still had their guns.

In a couple of hours a big truck drove through the main gate. In it was what appeared to be Americans and the colored parachutes we had seen earlier. After the truck pulled into the Japanese side of the camp, we began to worry. After several hours of no news our spirits began to droop.

The next day, the American colonel in charge of the rescue team was brought into our area and was allowed to talk to some of our senior officers. Yes, they were a rescue team, *but* the Japanese general of the Manchurian troops refused to surrender. So now what? Would we still be held?

Shortly after the American colonel talked with our senior officers, the American doctor with the team came onto our side and immediately conferred with our doctors and with the Japanese doctor. Their concern was for the very ill, and others needing urgent care.

In the meantime, we were told that atomic bombs had been dropped on Hiroshima and Nagasaki. Few of us understood the significance of the event until later, when we had time to assimilate all the things that had gone on in the world while we were out of circulation. It was then that we began to realize that, quite probably, if the bombs had not been dropped, many of us would never have been able to go home.

The next day the rest of the team was allowed to join us on our side. They included, in addition to the colonel and doctor, a Japanese interpreter, a Chinese interpreter and a Russian interpreter, as well as an expert in communications, with all of the needed equipment. Contact with American forces in China was begun immediately, the first order of business being to send the names and identification of all the surviving prisoners in the camp to the United States via U.S. forces in Kunming, China. The second order of business was to order food and medical supplies to be dropped in the camp. On the following day, American B-29s flew over the camp and parachutes filled with all kinds of food came raining down on the camp to the point where the pilots were told to back off a little, and to make their drops outside the camp.

It was too late, however, for one Japanese guard. One of the parachutes failed to open fully, and the load came down through the kitchen room, killing him. Everybody cheered.

On the following day, August 17, 1945, the Russians entered Mukden, and ended 39 months of captivity for me. The first thing that the Russian soldiers did was to relieve the Japanese of their weapons and give them to the Americans, who took over the job of protecting the Japanese prisoners. That was such a good thing to see.

The next few days were hectic. The sickest patients were examined by the rescue team doctor and the doctors who had been prisoners to determine priority for evacuation, which would have to be by air because the only railroad to the coast at Harbin had been bombed out, and it would be weeks before it could be repaired. Also the Mukden Airport was too small to accommodate the B-29s, meaning that the only American planes that could be used were the B-24s, which had a lot less space than the B-29s. Some B-24s were stripped of their armament, and red crosses were painted on the sides. A schedule was then set up for the evacuation of those who needed the most care. I was lucky enough to be able to get on a flight on the third or fourth day.

Before I left, though, small groups of prisoners were allowed to go into the city with Russian escorts, so I arranged for a trip as soon as I could, hoping I would not miss my plane. That trip was an experience. Our transportation was a horse-drawn, wagon-type passenger vehicle, since all the motorized equipment had been confiscated by the Russians.

The first stop was in the red light district because the Russian escort assumed that was where we wanted to go. As our vehicle approached the street the girls were standing in the doorways as far as we could see. As we turned on to the street, the girls just disappeared. Like mice scurrying for their holes, they vanished into thin air. No one in our group was disappointed, contrary to what the Russian escort thought.

Our next stop was at a Chinese restaurant, which we were much more interested in. We entered and sat down. When a Chinese man appeared, we asked for food as best we could. He began to wave frantically that he had no food. As he was trying to tell us that he had no food, the Russian escort brought his shouldered automatic weapon down in a quick sweep that started at the ceiling and ended at the floor, leaving several holes in the wall. The Chinese was long gone. Apparently he had had similar experiences under the Japanese.

Our escort then took us to the Mukden railroad depot, where thousands of Japanese were congregated by the Russians, either for repatriation home, or more likely for shipment to Russia as slave laborers. We were invited to help ourselves to anything the Japanese had that we might want. After considerable looking, I found that everything of value had been confiscated by the Russians or by Americans who had gotten there first. I eventually found a Japanese medic who had a medical aid kit which I took. I had a twinge of conscience, but the kit was nearly empty, so I didn't feel too badly about taking it.

We then headed back to camp to get something to eat. I had had enough of this war. I was ready to go home!

CHAPTER 17

At last the long awaited day had arrived. Freedom! Finally we would not have to stand muster anymore! No more having to salute a Japanese soldier or bow in their presence. No more empty stomachs and dehydrated bodies. There would be food for our skinny bodies, liquids to maintain our fluid balance, medicines to heal our sick bodies, and love instead of degradation, humiliation and brutality. No one in the world would appreciate freedom more than us.

Two weeks after the rescue team arrived at Camp Hoten, my journey to freedom began. Eight of us, all patients, left the camp enroute to the airport, where we were helped aboard a B-24. Because there were no seats (other than for the pilot and co-pilot), we were placed in spaces meant for bombs and other armaments. The bomb bay doors were secured, making room for some of us to lie down, and there were plenty of blankets for comfort. I found myself in the space usually occupied by the tail gunner, which was quite an experience for me, since that was my first ride on an aircraft.

Before we were ready for take-off, we were each issued a packet containing a "K" ration, prepared food with crackers, cookies, etc., to make a complete meal (it included four cigarettes). This was the forerunner of today's Army Meals Ready to Eat (MREs). As we took off, the pilot asked us if we would like to take a lasat look at the camp.

We all agreed, and the pilot swung the big plane around so he could make a low pass over the camp. Suddenly the plane made a steep climb, throwing those in the bomb bay toward the rear. We leveled off and the pilot apologized for the quick climb. He said that he did not see the tall smokestack at the camp, and had to take evasive action. So much for the first taste of freedom.

The rest of the trip we flew over some of the most beautiful mountainous land in the world. We flew over North China to Siam, the provisional capital of China. There we refueled and took off again. We had flown for about six hours, and we would have another four or five hours to go. Before we took off from Siam we were given another "K" ration.

The flight was uneventful, except that by the time we got to Kunming, China, most of us were very sick, with symptoms of nausea and cramping. It was so bad that we all had to be helped off the plane. We could not tolerate the food.

Kunming was the location of the advance Army base at the China end of the Burma Road, and it was inaccesible except by air (the Japanese occupied the territory from the coast inland). A large advance forward hospital was our first stop on the road to freedom. Our freedom was temporarily interrupted, however, when we were placed in isolation until we had all been physically examined. The next few days were spent getting innumerable tests and examinations including laboratory tests, X-rays, and physicals to determine our current state of health. Treatment was predicated on the findings of the tests, with priority given to those with communicable diseases and or acute conditions requiring immediate therapy. At this point I weighed 97 pounds. Since we had been getting better food during the last three months, I figured I might have been as low as 80 pounds. My weight before the war was 165 pounds. Two of the men had developed tuberculosis and were isolated for the remainder of the trip home. Those who had dysentery were started on medication. Those who had a history of malaria were instructed to promptly report any fever or chills. It would still take some time to get used to American food, but I was more than willing to try.

As soon as everyone had been cleared for travel, we were put aboard a DC-4 passenger plane along with other ex-prisoners who had been waiting. Each seat was filled. A few ex-prisoners were given an extra seat for comfort, and better access to help in case of emergency. There were three or four nurses and two or three doctors on board, and they were to stay with us until we arrived in the States. This was really first class travel.

The trip over the Himalayas was scary. There were mountains above us on both sides, and we were at a fair altitude. I'm glad that the trip was at night. I was able to sleep a little, so the fear subsided a bit. Early in the morning, we arrived at the airport in Calcutta, India, and were taken directly to the Army base hospital where we stayed several days. There were several POWs from other camps already there. They had been brought there for repatriation. I didn't know any of them, but they all had the same stories of starvation, brutality and illness.

At the Army hospital our group of enlisted men were assigned a full floor in one of the enlisted barracks while the officers in our group were housed in officer's quarters. We were told that we would be paid as soon as a record could be made for each of us, probably by the next day. We would also all be paid $500 apiece as an advance, and the remainder would be paid as soon as we were returned to our respective service. In the meantime, if we needed more money we need only to ask the paymaster of the unit to which we might be attached.

We were instructed to make ourselves available for debriefing during the next few days and that, for our convenience, the debriefing team would schedule our time. In the meantime we were instructed not to talk with anybody else about our experiences until we had been cleared. We were also told that we were free to go anywhere at any time, as long as we were available to meet the schedule for debriefing. All other base personnel were directed to stay clear of our barracks but that directive was not enforced.

Within a few hours of our arrival, an Army supply truck was parked at the entrance to the barracks. It was filled with nearly everything we could ever want in the line of food and beverages (nonalcoholic), and we were told that if we wanted anything that was not on the truck to just ask for it and the Army would do their best to provide it.

On the second day a few of the soldiers found their way into our quarters, despite the directive to stay away. Somehow the word had gotten out that we had been paid a large amount. Within a short time we were challenged to a poker game, and I was one of those who accepted the challenge. I won just a little less than $600. Twice in two days I had in my hand more money than I had ever had in my life.

While we were in Calcutta we attended several USO shows. I learned that the USO was an organization that provided entertainment to servicemen around the world, performing as close to the front as possible. Most of the famous screen stars, musicians and comedians traveled around the world many times to bring a little bit of home to the battle-weary men (and women). One of the shows I saw featured Fritz Kreisler, probably the world's finest violin player. Another show featured the Harmonicats, three extraordinary musicians with harmonicas.

Some of us ventured out into the city of Calcutta. I have never seen such poverty. Beggars lined the streets in some areas, and children (usually blind) were used to beg money, especially from the servicemen, who were very generous. We saw the hooded cobra act, in which the beggar plays a flute-like instrument while the cobra, tied by a string, rises slowly from a covered basket and sways with the music. Another act involved the cobra and the little mongoose which is a deadly enemy of the cobra. In that act the mongoose is allowed to attack the cobra but is quickly withdrawn from the fray before the cobra can be hurt.

All the time I was in Calcutta, I heard nothing from my wife. I was concerned but I was sure that she would be found before I got back to the States. I was assured that the Navy, as well as the Bureau of Missing Persons and the Red Cross, would make every effort to find her. I was not ready to panic yet.

On the sixth day we were readied for travel again and were put aboard another DC-4, with the same team of doctors and nurses we had had on the trip over the Himalayas. We took off late on a moonlit evening, and a short time later flew over the Taj Mahal, a magnificent sight. Early in the morning we arrived at Karachi, India, where we stayed for two days. In Karachi I visited the zoo, and walked around the city, which, like Calcutta, had pockets of abject poverty everywhere. These contrasted with areas of lavishness, ornate buildings, and large cars. Nearly everywhere I went somebody was trying to sell something. I finally bought a beautiful ruby ring to give to my wife. When I got home the ring had turned green, and a jeweler said that the "ruby" was only glass.

The Red Cross reported that there was still no word from my wife Bobbie. I was still confident that she would be located. In Calcutta, I had given the Red Cross the name of my sister Louella (Toni) as family contact, but I had no idea where she might be.

After two days of mostly boredom, we boarded our DC-4, and after a hassle with some senior officer trying to board our plane, we took off. The pilot had been ordered not to allow anyone on this plane, regardless of rank, except the POWs and the doctors and nurses assigned to the plane.

Our take-off was early in the morning, and we arrived in Iran about noon. We had only a short stay there, but we were offered an opportunity to get off the plane and stretch if we wanted. I stepped down the ramp and onto the tarmac, took two steps and my feet were on fire. The temperature must have been 120°F. I couldn't get back on the plane fast enough. About an hour later we took off again, and a very short time later, we landed at another unknown airport in Iraq. This time I had no desire to get off the plane.

After about an hour in Iraq, we took off again and landed later that afternoon in Cairo, Egypt. In Cairo we were taken to a British barracks where we were treated very well. British soldiers escorted us to all the sights in and around Cairo. I saw the Royal Mosque atop a large hill in the center of Cairo. I visited the Sphinx, the pyramids and a number of museums. As I recall, we were here for about four days.

By this time, the Red Cross was concerned that they still could not locate either my wife or my sister. They assured me that they would continue to keep on trying. I began to feel a little like a sole survivor.

One evening we again boarded our DC-4 with the same doctors and nurses. So far, there had not been any emergencies or problems, and everybody, even the most ill, was enjoying the tour around the world. As we left the lights of Cairo, most of us were tired from all the activity and we fell asleep easily. I was awakened about midnight to find that we were on the ground at the airport in Tunis, Tunisia, and before I could get oriented, we were off again.

In the early morning we landed at the airport at Casablanca, Morocco, on the west coast of North Africa. As we left the plane, we were advised that we would probably be staying until the next day. We could look around if we wanted, but we should keep in touch with our unit at the airport because our plane might leave earlier. I spent a few hours in the city which exhibited the same poverty that I had seen in Calcutta, Kaurachi, Pakistan, and Cairo. I ran across a barber shop and decided to get a haircut. Just as I was getting into the chair, one of the guys in our group spotted me and told me that word had just been passed that our plane was leaving in about four hours. If I didn't want to make that flight, there would be another flight the next day. Because I liked the group I was with, particularly the medical personnel, I wanted to stay on the same plane, if possible. So I made haste back to the airport and reported in.

About dusk we took off from the Casablanca Airport and headed in a westerly direction, landing at an airport in the Azores about midnight. Since this was only a refueling stop, we did not have an opportunity to see anything. As soon as we were ready, the plane took off and I resumed my sleep.

When I awoke, the plane was on the ground again, this time in Hamilton, Bermuda. What a beautiful sight. I knew that Bermuda was not far from the American mainland, and I began to feel the thrill of going home after a long time. This stop too, was only for refueling, and we were soon on our way. I began to get excited and had a hard time being patient. My anxiety turned momentarily to fear as the pilot dragged the tail of the plane on the takeoff. The plane shuddered, then finally left the runway for the clear sky.

About noon the plane settled down on a runway at the airport at Miami, Florida! Words cannot explain the feeling I had when I looked down on American soil. What a thrill! On September 28, 1945, six years, four months, and three days after I left San Francisco, I was home at last. All of us gave a big cheer before we got off the plane, and gave thanks to the medical personnel who had been so good to us for so long. There were tears in my eyes as I stepped down off the flight steps. I quickly knelt down and said "thank you, thank you" to somebody "up there" who had been looking out for me.

From the airport, we were bussed to the Naval hospital in Miami, which was located in one of the luxury resort hotels. By the time we all were checked in and assigned to wards, it was late afternoon and too late to get clothing to replace the Army khaki shirt and pants, with the olive drab underwear issued to us at Kunming, China. The commanding officer of the hospital greeted us and assured us that we would not be there for very long, only long enough for the respective services to process our papers and arrange for our transfer to military facilities of our choice. We would go home as quickly as possible.

Another fellow and I decided that we wanted a taste of real freedom, so with no uniform and no liberty card we headed for the main entrance. The sharp Marine sentry at the gate stopped us and told us that there was no way we could leave the building without being in uniform and having a liberty card. After a few words, we convinced the sentry to call the commanding officer, which he did. After the call, he said that he was told, "You had better let them go." He did, scratching his head in wonderment. We proceeded on through the door, walked for about a block or so, then turned around and went back to the hotel (hospital).

The next day I was flown to the Naval hospital at Jacksonville, Florida, by a small Beechcraft, four-passenger plane. At Jacksonville, I went immediately to the Red Cross to ask if they had located my wife or my sister. A few hours later they contacted me, with both bad news and good news. The good news was that they had located my sister and my mother. The bad news was that my wife had not been located yet, but they were still trying. I called my sister and told her that I was back home, and that I would appreciate it if she would call mother and tell her.

The following day, while permanent records were being updated, I went to small stores for uniforms and supplies. I was tired of Army khaki. The first hurdle I met was with uniforms. I was a second class pharmacist's mate when I was captured and was given one rating retroactive to the date of capture. According to the personnel officer, I should expect to be promoted to chief pharmacist's mate as soon as my records were completed. The question was whether I should buy the bell bottom and jumper suits or opt for the chief's uniform at the risk of not making the higher rate. I chose to take the chance and bought just one chief's uniform, together with underwear, shoes, socks, and a host of toilet articles. Since I was still a long way from my prewar weight, I made sure that I got an extra size or two in my uniform so that I could grow into it. I felt like I was back in the service again, at last.

The second day I met a very close friend. He and I had served together at the Naval Hospital, Newport, Rhode Island, from 1935 to 1939. We had shared many good times together. We had dated girls who were very close friends. He had married his girlfriend in 1938, and my girlfriend and I attended his wedding, she as bridesmaid, and I as best man. For the next few days we spent a lot of time catching up on the past. I found out from him that my old girlfriend's sister had married a Navy chief and they were living on base. My friend took me to see them, and I immediately got in touch with my old girlfriend. We had a long talk.

Within a week my chief pharmacist's mate rating came through, and I bought a full set of both blues and khakis. I then was asked where I would like to go for duty. I said, "Right here," and I became a member of the staff at Jacksonville Naval Hospital.

There was still no word from my wife, and I was beginning to get discouraged. I had 90 days' leave coming, but I wasn't sure where I should go on leave, or whether I should wait longer to see if they could find her. I finally decided not to wait any longer. I drew my leave papers and took off for Detroit to visit with my family. I was pleasantly surprised at the reunion. My mother and Uncle Charlie (who was in the Army in World War I) met me at the train station, and drove me to Mother's, where, within a few days, I visited with nearly all my family.

It was then that I learned that my brother Russell, who had gone in the Navy just before the war started, had been on the *Arizona* at Pearl Harbor when it was sunk. He survived, but at a cost to his mental health. My youngest brother had enlisted in the Army and was at that time still in Italy, with Patton's Army. Mother was a Gold Star mother and was most proud that she had three sons in the service. When Jim got home it was a great day, the first time we had been together for a lot of years.

For the first month or more in Detroit, I was frequently reminded that the nation was still experiencing rationing. Meat and sugar were the rationed items I noticed first, since they were two of the items I missed most in prison camp. Since I had no ration card, I was not able to help my mother get the things I wanted most. But with family help, she was able to help feed my insatiable appetite. I found it incredible that, after starving for three and one-half years, I did not have a ration card for food when I got home. On one occasion, I stopped at a drug store and asked for a chocolate-marshmallow sundae. The old man behind the counter said that he didn't have any of the three ingredients, then added, "Son, don't you know there has been a war on?" I thought for a second, then reached over and grabbed a napkin holder and threw it in his direction. I did not wait around for what might have happened. I was too mad to be reasonable.

During the rest of September and part of October 1945, I had little opportunity to enjoy my freedom or my family. From the day my picture appeared in a Detroit paper, I was deluged with letters and telephone calls, most of them inquiring about a family member or loved one. Did I know them? If I knew them, did I know what happened to them? I did my best to answer their questions, because I knew how desperate they were for any kind of information.

I eventually became so tired that I had to get away. I did not want to relive that nightmare several times a day. There was still no word from my wife. I had nearly given up. It was entirely possible that she might not be alive. Something might have happened to her. It had been a long, long time.

To escape for a while, I decided to go to Newport, Rhode Island, and visit some friends (including my old girlfriend). After about a week in Newport, I developed a fever that sent me to the Naval hospital there. The diagnosis was acute pyelonephritis (a severe kidney infection). My temperature was high enough that I wasn't aware of what was happening. In a few days my temperature was down, and I began to complain about the penicillin shots in the hip every four hours. I was now aware that I was in the same room in the hospital ward where I had taken care of patients several years before.

After three weeks, I was well enough to leave the hospital, and I returned to Detroit to continue my leave. Things were much quieter now. The telephone didn't keep ringing and there were fewer letters.

I was able to spend the Christmas holidays with Mother and others in the family, my first real Christmas in five years. While I was going with a nice girl, I somehow felt lonely. It would have been much better if I had known what happened to my wife. The first week in January, I decided that I had waited long enough for my wife to be found. Three months had passed without a clue as to her whereabouts. I contacted a lawyer (whom I had known in Cabanatuan) and filed for divorce on the grounds of desertion. There was one positive thing about the whole situation, though. In December, when my pay records had finally been reconciled, I discovered that all the allotment checks to her had been returned. At the start of the war we were advised that, if we hadn't done so already, we should make out an allotment to our next of kin. I made mine out for all my pay. In looking back over the situation, I feel that because I was listed as missing, and presumed dead, she had given me up, and was honest enough to be fair about the allotment. I discovered, after I returned, that the Navy Department still listed me as a crew member of the USS *Sealion* (it was sunk at the Cavite Navy Yard on the first day of the war).

The second week in January I developed another fever and reported to the Navy dispensary in Detroit where arrangements were made for my transfer to the Naval Hospital at Greak Lakes, Illinois. When I left my mother's home that day, she put all the letters I had received in my suitcase in case I might be interested in answering any of them.

Within a few days, the fever was gone, and I was back to near normal. The only persistent problem that I had was that my legs were still weak, and I had to be careful how and where I walked. While I was lying in bed at Great Lakes, I went through some of the letters in my suitcase. I intended to someday answer them all. One of the letters caught my attention. It was from a Helen Dorothy Gonser, and it bore a Chicago address. As soon as I was able to go on liberty, I got her telephone number from information, and gave her a call. I told her who I was and asked if I could take her to dinner that night (it was Saturday). Her reply was to the effect that she would go to dinner with me if she could bring along her sister and brother-in-law. I agreed to that arrangement, and asked if she could recommend a hotel where I might be able to get a room. It was virtually impossible to get a hotel room without a reservation. She said that she would have her brother-in-law get me a reservation in a downtown hotel, and he would call to tell me where.

That night was one of the highlights of my life. Helen turned out to be the ideal woman, and it wasn't long before we were sure that we wanted to share our lives together.

My leave was about to expire, and I decided that I would like to be stationed in Chicago, instead of Jacksonville, Florida. The Navy agreed, and assigned me to the Naval Recruiting Station in Chicago. On July 27, 1946, Helen and I were married at the Navy Pier, in Chicago, by a Navy chaplain. Shortly after we were married, I was promoted to commissioned warrant officer and transferred to Great Lakes Naval Hospital for duty. Except for one year at the Navy Hospital Administration School in Bethesda, Md., I stayed at Great Lakes until a heart attack nearly ended my career. After that experience the Navy sent me to the School of Environmental Health, in Oakland, California.

After three years at Point Mugu, California, I was given a choice of three duty stations for transfer: Hawaii, Japan, or the Philippines. After considerable thinking, I chose to go back to the Philippines.

In November of 1959, I was given orders to retire. My military career was over. My journey ended.

APPENDIX

*Roster of Naval Medical
Department Personnel in
the Asiatic-Pacific Theater 1941–1945*

Following is a roster of Navy medical department personnel on duty in the Far East (except Guam, and Wake and Midway Islands) at the outset of World War II. Their assignments included the Naval Hospital, Canacao, the dispensaries at the Navy Yard, Cavite, and Naval Station, Olongapo, in the Philippines, and various units of the Fourth Regiment, U.S. Marines in the Philippines and China. This roster does not include Navy medical personnel attached to the various ships of the Asiatic Fleet which was able to escape the Japanese onslaught. The USS *Canopus* and several auxilliary ships, which were unable to accompany the fleet, were scuttled prior to the surrender. The names of medical personnel on those units are contained herein.

The accuracy of the information contained in this roster is questionable only to the extent that the sources of information are not official, but they are reliable. For this reason I consider the information contained in these pages to be the best available. I apologize for any errors the reader might find. I am deeply grateful for the sources of this information to Ernest J. Irvin, Robert W. Kentner, and Cecil J. Peart, all former shipmates and fellow POWs, and to Jan Herman, historian for the Navy Department Bureau of Medicine and Surgery for his help in providing historical data for this manuscript.

The following medical personnel died on the *Oryoku Maru* in Subic Bay, Philippines, or on the *Enuora Maru* in Takao Harbor, Formosa.

Name	Rank/Rate	Assignment
BANSLEY, Donald E.	PhM2c	4th Reg. Marines
BARRETT, Arthur M.	LT MC	USS *Mindanao*
BECK, Louis G.	CPhM	USS *Mindanao*
BJURLING, Eldon W.	PhM1c	USNH Canacao
BOONE, James D.	LCDR MC	USNH Canacao
BOWLIN, Seldon C.	PhM3c	USNH Canacao
BYRD, Jack R.	PhM1c	USS *Canopus*
COMPTON, Luther C.	PhM2c	USNH Canacao
CONDON, Clifford K.	WO HC	USNH Canacao
CONNELL, James A.	LCDR DC	USS *Otus*
DARLING, James H.	PhM2c	USS *Canopus*
DAVIS, Thomas A.	PhM3c	Dispensary, Olongapo
DECKER, James R.	PhM1c	4th Reg. Marines
DUNN, William D.	HA1c	USNH Canacao
EDWARDS, George D.	PhM2c	USS *Canopus*
GOING, Roland E.	PhM2c	USNH Canacao
GOMES, Abel O.	CPhM	USNH Canacao
GORDON, Harvey	PhM1c	4th Reg. Marines
HASTINGS, Edward W.	CPhM	USS *Canopus*
HAYES, Thomas H.	CDR MC	USNH Canacao
HENSEN, Dudley A.	PhM2c	USNH Canacao
HOGAN, Emmett O.	WO HC	USNH Canacao
HOGSHIRE, George W.	LCDR MC	Dispensary, Olongapo
JONES, Howard M.	PhM1c	USS *Asheville*
JOSES, Maurice	CDR MC	4th Reg. Marines
JOYNER, Henry C.	HA1c	USNH Canacao
KERBOW, Harry J.	CPhM	USS *Otus*
LAMBERT, Gordon K.	LT MC	Dispensary, Cavite
LAVICTOIRE, Isaac N.	LT MC	USNH Canacao
LECONTE, Charles F.	LT MC	USS *Canopus*
MAASS, Adolph R.	WO HC	USS *Bittern*

Name	Rank/Rate	Assignment
McCURRY, Dennah R.	PhM3c	USNH Canacao
MacDOUGALL, Daniel	HMIC	Dispensary, Casvite
MAYBERRY, Richard H.	PhM2c	USNH Canacao
MORGAN, Jack P.	PhM1c	4th Reg. Marines
MUNROE, William L.	PhM1c	USNH Canacao
NELSON, Edward R.	LT MC	Dispensary, Cavite
NEY, Ralph S.	PhM3c	4th Reg. Marines
NICHOLSON, Bruce	CPhM	USS *Luzon*
RITTER, Edward F.	LT MC	USS *Trinity*
SANDERS, Fred R.	PhM2c	USNH Canacao
SCHWEICK, Jerome J.	HA1c	USNH Canacao
SCHNABEL, Charles W.	CPhM	USS *Canopas*
SIMMONS, Dorris P.	CPhM	4th Reg. Marines
SLIPSAGER, Glenn E.	PhM1c	USS *Finch*
THOMPSON, Walter N.	PhM2c	USNH Canacao
TURNIPSEED, Jess	WO HC	USNH Canacao
ULMER, John C.	CPhM	USS *Dahn*
WADE, Ernest	LCDR MC	4th Reg. Marines
WELCH, Cecil C.	LCDR MC	USNH Canacao
WELSH, Clyde L.	LCDR MC	USNH Canacao
WHITE, Alfred F.	LT DC	USNH Canacao
WILSON, James, M.	PhM1c	USNH Canacao
WRIGHT, Edgar B.	PhM1c	Dispensary, Cavite

The following medical personnel survived the war and were repatriated from Japan.

Name	Rank/Rate	Assignment
COBURN, Dean A.	PhM2c	USNH Canacao
CREWS, Jeremiah V.	WO HC	4th Reg. Marines
CROWELL, George W.	PhM1c	USNH Canacao
DERRICK, William T.	PhM1c	Dispensary, Cavite
DODSON, Merrill E.	HA1c	USNH Canacao
GORDON, Carl B.	PhM1c	Dispensary, Cavite
HAASE, Edward F.	WO HC	Dispensary, Cavite
HAGSTROM, Alfred S.	PhM2c	4th Reg. Marines
ISTOCK, John T.	PhM2c	USNH Canacao
LYNCH, Roy E.	PhM1c	4th. Reg. Marines
MAXWELL, Frank L.	PhM1c	USS *Napa*
MYERS, Estel B.	HA1c	USNH Canacao
RAPP, Floyd C.	HA1c	USNH Canacao

Name	Rank/Rate	Assignment
ROGERS, Eugene F.	HA1c	USNH Canacao
TAPPY, Lester R.	PhM3c	USNH Canacao
TAPSCOTT, Donald E.	PhM2c	USNH Canacao
TYBUR, Albert J.	PhM1c	4th Reg. Marines
VERNON, John F.	PhM1c	USNH Canacao

The following medical personnel survived the war and were repatriated from Manchuria.

Name	Rank/Rate	Assignment
COOK, Collins W.	PhM3c	USNH Canacao
FAST, Chester K.	HA1c	USNH Canacao
FRALEIGH, Claud M.	LT DC	USS *Canopus*
LANGDON, B.B.	LT MC	NSNH Canacao
PEART, Cecil J.	PhM2c	4th Reg. Marines
SMITH, Carey M.	CDR	USNH Canacao
STAMP, Loren E.	PhM2c	USS *Canopus*
THOMPSON, Robert E.	PhM1c	USS *Canopus*

The following medical personnel died on other ships enroute to Japan.

Name	Rank/Rate	Assignment
AMBRO, Eugene A.	PhM2c	USS *Canopus*
ANDERSON, Irwin H.	PhM2c	USNH Canacao
ARNOLD, George M.	PhM3c	USNH Canacao
AVERY, Roy E.	HA2c	Dispensary, Cavite
BAER, Robert W.	HA2c	USNH Canacao
BLANCETT, Jesse R.	PhM3c	4th Reg. Marines
BLAYDES, Wilbur K.	PhM3c	4th Reg. Marines
BLOOMINGDALE, Leslie F.	HA1c	4th Reg. Marines
BROHMAN, Henry C.	PhM1c	4th Reg. Marines
BYRD, Hershel W.	PhM3c	4th Reg. Marines
CARAWAN, Bonega C.	PhM3c	4th Reg. Marines
CAREY, Jerry D.	PhM3c	USNH Canacao
CHRISTENSEN, Ernest L.	PhM3c	USNH Canacao
COLLINS, Fred E.	CPhM	USNH Canacao
DAVIS, David W.	PhM3c	USNH Canacao
DEMUTH, Paul V.	PhM3c	USNH Canacao
DIAZ, Arthur T.	CPhM	USS *Seadragon*
DICK, Robert J.	PhM3c	USNH Canacao

Name	Rank/Rate	Assignment
DONEHUE, William E.	PhM3c	Dispensary, Cavite
DURHAM, Irvin W.	HA1c	USNH Canacao
FERGUSON, George T.	LT MC	USNH Canacao
FLEMING, Kenneth E.	PhM1c	USNH Canacao
FRANCIS, Lloyd J.	PhM3c	USNH Canacao
FRASIER, Clarence A.	CPhM	Dispensary, Cavite
FULLER, Eddy W.	PhM3c	USNH Canacao
FULTON, Judson P.	PhM2c	Dispensary, Cavite
GALLAHER, Robert N.	PhM3c	Dispensary, Cavite
GARDELLA, Francis A.	PhM3c	USNH Canacao
GASPA, Leonard J.	PhM2c	USNH Canacao
GLICK, David A.	PhM3c	USNH Canacao
GLOVER, Herbert P.	PhM2c	4th Reg. Marines
GODWIN, Luther H.	PhM3c	4th Reg. Marines
GUTHRIE, George T.	PhM3c	USNH Canacao
HALWEG, Stanley M.	PhM3c	USNH Canacao
HARRINGTON, Edward D.	PhM2c	Dispensary, Cavite
HARTZ, William A.	PhM3c	USNH Canacao
HELMS, William A.	PhM2c	Dispensary, Cavite
HEMPLEMAN, William V.	HA1c	USNH Canacao
HETZLER, Marvin L.	PhM2c	Dispensary, Cavite
HOOVER, John H.	PhM2c	4th Reg. Marines
HOYLE, Jack M.	PhM3c	USNH Canacao
JANNEY, General A.	PhM3c	USNH Canacao
JAY, John P.	PhM3c	USNH Canacao
JENKINS, Jack W.	PhM3c	Dispensary, Cavite
JUNKER, Dana S.	PhM2c	USNH Canacao
KELLY, Shirley H.	PhM2c	USNH Canacao
KING, Orville W.	PhM3c	4th Reg. Marines
KIRBY, Henry L.	PhM2c	USNH Canacao
KLUMKER, George G.	PhM2c	USNH Canacao
KOEHLER, Ralph C.	PhM1c	USNH Canacao
KRUMHOLZ, William A.	PhM3c	USNH Canacao
LINVILLE, Jess Jr.	PhM3c	Dispensary, Cavite
McCLATCHEY, Virgil F.	PhM3c	USNH Canacao
McCLENDON, Darwin A.	PhM3c	USNH Canacao
McKINNON, Richard L.	PhM3c	USNH Canacao
MARIETTE, Maxwell A.	PhM2c	4th Reg. Marines
MARSHALL, William L.	PhM3c	USNH Canacao
MATHESON, Roy L.	HA1c	USNH Canacao

Name	Rank/Rate	Assignment
MILLER, Charles E.	Sea1c	USS *Finch*
NOYES, Elton L.	PhM1c	USNH Canacao
PARKER, Arthur R.	CPhM	Dispensary, Cavite
PEACHY, Gerald R.	PhM3c	USNH Canacao
PERCIFUL, Victor F.	PhM1c	USNH Canacao
PHILSON, Clark A.	HA1c	USNH Canacao
PLILER, Luther M.	CPhM	USNH Canacao
POWELL, Odeen D.	PhM3c	USS *Canopus*
PRANGE, Edward H.	PhM2c	4th Reg. Marines
PROFFIT, Leonard	PhM3c	USNH Canacao
RICE, Jack	PhM3c	USNH Canacao
RIHN, James J.	PhM1c	USNH Canacao
RIKER, Dorman N.	PhM2c	USNH Canacao
SANFORD, Tebe D., Jr.	PhM3c	USNH Canacao
SHILLINGTON, Thomas W.	HA1c	USNH Canacao
SHIPMAN, Wesley E.	HA1c	USNH Canacao
SHUMWAY, Kenneth W.	PhM2c	USS *Canopus*
SPARKMAN, Eldon E.	CPhM	Dispensary, Olongapo
SPEISS, Norman J.	PhM3c	Dispensary, Olongapo
STANDEFER, John Y.	PhM3c	4th Reg. Marines
STEVENS, James J.	PhM1c	USNH Canacao
STEWART, Russell C.	PhM3c	Dispensary, Cavite
STUEVE, Emmett G.	PhM3c	Dispensary, Cavite
TAYLOR, Forest L.	PhM2c	USS *Canopus*
TURNER, Kenneth E.	PhM2c	USNH Canacao
TYREE, Lawrence F.	PhM2c	USS *Canopus*
VINCENT, Claud M.	PhM2c	Dispensary, Olongapo
VISE, William G.	HA1c	USNH Canacao
WAWRZONEK, Louis J.	PhM3c	4th Reg. Marines
WELLS, Arthur, Jr.	PhM1c	USS *Pecos*
WENDROFF, Robert	HA1c	USNH Canacao

The following medical personnel were killed in action during the fighting in the Philippines.

Name	Rank/Rate	Assignment
ALLEN, George R.	PhM3c	USNH *Canacao*—KIA Cavite
BAIR, Frederick F.	PhM3c	USNH *Canacao*—KIA Corregidor

126

Name	Rank/Rate	Assignment
LANEY, Edward A.	PhM2c	Dispensary Cavite—KIA Cavite
LYONS, Edward F.	PhM2c	USNH Canacao—KIA Cavite
OLSON, Kermonth N.	PhM3c	Dispensary Cavite—KIA Cavite
RICH, Otto V.	PhM1c	USNH Canacao—KIA Cavite
RUCHINSKY, Stephen	PhM1c	USNH Canacao—KIA Cavite

The following were killed in the Palawan Massacre in the Philippines when the Japanese made the prisoners dig a pit, and crawl into it. They poured fuel oil over them and set them on fire. There were few survivors.

Name	Rank/Rate	Assignment
HUNT, Jack E.	PhM3c	4th Reg. Marines
KNIGHT, W. E.	LT DC	4th Reg. Marines

The following medical personnel survived prison camp and were repatriated from Japan (or from China, where they were captured when left there in 1941).

Name	Rank/Rate	Assignment
ALVERSON, Lloyd H.	PhM3c	USNH Canacao
BELL, Bernard R.	HA1c	USNH Canacao
BERLEY, Ferdinand V.	LT MC	Dispensary, Cavite
BJORNSTAD, Royce B.	HA2c	USNH Canacao
BLACK, Loy J.	HA1c	Repatriated from Peking
BOLSTER, Richard L.	CPhM	USS *Pigeon*
BOOKMAN, John J.	LT MC	Mariveles
BRADLEY, Joseph J.	PhM3c	USNH Canacao
BROKENSHIRE, Herbert C.	LT MC	USNH Canacao
CASSADY, Frank L.	HA1c	USNH Canacao
CASSETTE, James L.	PhM3c	Lanikai
CASTEEL, Lacey L.	CPhM	USS *Tanager*
CAWEIN, Richard O.	PhM3c	USNH Canacao

Name	Rank/Rate	Assignment
CHAMBERLIN, Russell D.	PhM3c	4th Reg. Marines
CLOUGH, James B.	PhM3c	USNH Canacao
COWAN, Alva R.	CPhM	Dispensary, Cavite
CRAWFORD, Robert C.	PhM3c	USNH Canacao
CURRIE, Frank	HA1c	Dispensary, Cavite
DAVIS, Herman	PhM3c	4th Reg. Marines— Tientsin
DEGROAT, Dudley E.	HA1c	USNH Canacao
DITCH, William I.	PhM3c	4th Reg. Marines
DIXON, George R.	PhM2c	4th Reg. Marines
ECKSTEIN, Leon W.	PhM2c	USNH Canacao
ERICKSON, Hjalmer A.	LCDR MC	Dispensary, Cavite
FLOOD, Donald R.	PhM2c	4th Reg. Marines
FOX, Edwin S.	PhM1c	Repatriated from Peiping
FUENTES, Maximo D.	CPhM	USS *Genessee*
GEORGE, Jack R.	LT MC	USNH Canacao
GLUSMAN, Murray	LT MC	Dispensary, Cavite
GOODWIN, William R.	PhM3c	4th Reg. Marines
GREENMAN, Robert B.	LT MC	USS *Oahu*
HALL, Ellison K.	CPhM	Repatriated from Peking
HARRIS, Charles W.	PhM3c	USNH Canacao
HEAD, George W.	CPhM	Escaped from Cor- regidor on USS *Quail*
HERTHNECK, Robert G.	LT DC	USNH Canacao
HILDEBRAND, Bernard V.	PhM2c	USNH Canacao
HOOD, Winton C.	PhM2c	USNH Canacao
HUNT, William S.	PhM1c	Repatriated from Peiping
IRVIN, Ernest J.	PhM2c	4th Reg. Marines
JOHNSON, Earl R.	HA1c	Repatriated from Peiping
LOCKLEAR, Thomas E.	PhM3c	USNH Canacao
LUTHER, John H.	PhM2c	USNH Canacao
MacBAIN, Arthur G.	PHM1c	USS *Canopus*
MacDOUGALL, Daniel	PHM1c	Dispensary, Cavite
MANSON, Emmett L.	LT DC	Dispensary, Olongapo
MOFFETT, Kenneth P.	PhM2c	USNH Canacao (Sur-

Name	Rank/Rate	Assignment
		vived the Bataan Death March)
MORGAN, Wade H.	LT DC	Dispensary, Cavite
NARDINI, John	LT MC	4th Reg. Marines
NELSON, Harold R.	PhM3c	4th Reg. Marines
NICHOLSON, Bruce M.	CPhM	USS *Luzon*
OVERLY, Clyde H.	PhM2c	VP Sq. 101
PARKER, Arthur R.	PhM3c	Dispensary, Cavite
PATTON, Ralph E.	PhM3c	USNH Canacao
PFEIFFER, James R.	WO HC	USNH Canacao
RILEY, William E.	PhM1c	4th Reg. Marines
RYAN, John F.	PhM3c	Repatriated from Tientsin
SCHRAEDER, Arthur H.	PhM3c	Repatriated from Tientsin
SMITH, Stanley W.	LT DC	Dispensary, Cavite
STEEL, Walter E.	CPhM	USNH Canacao
STRADLEY, Bernard T.	PhM2c	USNH Canacao
STRANGMAN, William L.	LT DC	4th Reg. Marines
TAYLOR, Forest L.	PhM2c	USS *Canopus*
TRUAX, John S.	PhM3c	USNH Canacao
WADE, Thomas J.	CPhM1	USS *Napa*
WADLEY, Edward D.	PhM3c	USNH Canacao
WALLACE, Richard D.	PhM3c	USNH Canacao
WALMER, Edgar B.	PhM2c	Repatriated from Peiping
WANGER, James L.	LT DC	USS *Houston*

The following medical personnel were repatriated from Manchuria, where all senior officers had been interned early after the surrender.

Name	Rank/Rate	Assignment
DAVIS, Robert C.	CAPT MC	USNH Canacao
LOWMAN, Kenneth E.	CAPT MC	Fleet Surgeon
ROBERTS, Lyle J.	CAPT MC	USNH Canacao

The following medical personnel survived prison camp and were repatriated from Bilibid, Cabanatuan, or from China, where they had been left when the 4th Marines evacuated China in 1941.

Name	Rank/Rate	Assignment
BRANNON, Thomas F., Jr.	PhM2c	USNH Canacao
BRAY, James F., Jr.	PhM2c	4th Reg. Marines

Name	Rank/Rate	Assignment
CASTLETON, John V.	PhM1c	Repatriated from China
CROSS, Cornelius T.	LCdr MC	USNH Canacao
FARR, Morris C.	PhM3c	Dispensary, Olongapo
FUENTES, Maximo D.	CPhM	USS *Genesee*
HARTWELL, Clarence V.	PhM3c	USNH Canacao
KENTNER, Robert W.	PhM2c	USNH Canacao
KLINE, Edward F.	LT MC	USS *Marblehead*
NOVAK, Louis, Jr.	PhM2c	4th Reg. Marines
PAYNE, Harry L.	PhM3c	4th Reg. Marines
PERMENTER, Donald O.	PhM3c	USNH Canacao
POHLMAN, Max E.	LT MC	USS *Canopus*
SARTIN, Lea B.	CDR MC	USNH Canacao
SHEARER, Clarence	WO HC	USNH Canacao
SILLIPHANT, William M.	LT MC	USNH Canacao
SMITH, Alfred L.	LT MC	USS *Luzon*
WARE, Ralph G.	PhM2c	USNH Canacao
ZUNDELL, Joseph L.	LCDR MC	USS *Otus*

Following is a list of Navy nurses who were on duty at the Naval Hospital, Canacao, when the war started. When the Japanese occupied Manila these nurses were interned in Santo Thomas University, Manila, from where they were repatriated early in 1942. The omission from my manuscript of the role of the Navy nurses was intentional only because I had no knowledge of their experiences after I left Manila with the Marines in mid–December, 1941. This does not mean that they did not make a significant contribution to the war effort. There is no question that they were a significant part of the Navy Medical Department. These nurses were officially *internees*, not prisoners of war. Their treatment at the hands of the Japanese was usually less severe than that of other medical personnel. This is not to say that they did not suffer as much from malnutrition, disease and the effects of incarceration.

Name	Rank
BERNATITUS, Ann A.*	Nurse Corps
CHAPMAN, Mary F.	Nurse Corps
COBB, Lauea M.	Nurse Corps

*This Navy nurse was transferred to Bataan early in the war, and then to Corregidor, from where she was evacuated, with several Army nurses, by submarine to Australia. She was never a POW, or Internee.

Name	Rank
EVANS, Bertha A.	Nurse Corps
GORZELANSKY, Helen C.	Nurse Corps
HARRINGTON, Mary R.	Nurse Corps
NASH, Margaret A.	Nurse Corps
O'HAVER, Goldie A.	Nurse Corps
PAIGE, Eldene F.	Nurse Corps
PITCHER, Susie J.	Nurse Corps
STILL, Dorothy	Nurse Corps
TODD, C. Edwina	Nurse Corps

A total of 277 Navy Medical Department personnel were on duty in the Philippines (and China) when the war started. Of those, 154 died (only 7 during the fighting), for a death rate of over 55 percent. This is an exceptionally high death rate for noncombatants.

Of the 1619 prisoners who started the trip to Japan on the *Oryoku Maru*, 81 were Navy Medical Department personnel. Of those Navy doctors and hospital corpsmen, 57 died as a result of American air attacks, either on the *Oryoku Maru* or the *Enoura Maru*. Many died of wounds and 24 survived and were repatriated.

Ninety-four more Navy medical personnel died on other ships enroute to Japan, or in prison camps in Japan. Many more died of malnutrition and or mistreatment.

BIBLIOGRAPHY

For those who seek more information about the starvation, cruelty and subhuman conditions under the Japanese military, these books are a must, and I highly recommend them.

Abraham, Abie, MSgt, AUS (ret). *Ghost of Bataan Speaks*. New York: Vantage Press, 1971.

Ashton, Paul, M.D. *And Somebody Gives a Damn*. Santa Barbara, CA: Ashton, 1990.

_____. *Bataan Diary*. Santa Barbara, CA: Ashton, 1985.

Bergee, Lee K. *Guest of the Emperor—The Personal Story of Frank Promnitz, USMC*. High Ridge, MO: Four Freedoms Press, 1987.

Brown, Charles M., Lt. Col. AUS Ret. *The Oryoku Maru Story*. Magalia, CA: Unpublished.

Craig, J. B. "Stoney," *Corregidor and Beyond—Recollections of a Japanese POW for 3½ Years, and More*. Pittsfield, IL: Unpublished.

Evans, William R. *SOOCHOW and the Fourth Marines*. Rogue River, OR: Springs Printery, 1987.

Harrison, Thomas R. *Survivor—Memoirs of Defeat and Captivity, Bataan 1942*. Salt Lake City, UT: Western Epics, 1989.

Hayes, Thomas, Cdr. MC, USN. *Bilibid Diary*. Hamden, CT: Shoe String Press, 1987.

Jackfert, Edward and Andrew Miller. *History of the Defenders of the Philippines, Guam and Wake, Is.* Paducah, KY: Turner, 1991.

133

Jacobs, Eugene, Col. MC, AUS (Ret). *Blood Brothers—A Medic's Sketchbook*. New York: Carlton Press, 1985.

Kentner, R. W. *Kentner's Journal*. Bureau of Medicine and Surgery Archives, 1948.

Kirek, Terrence S. *The Secret Camera*. Cotati, CA: LaBoheme, 1983.

Lawton, Manny. *Some Survived*. Chapel Hill, NC: Algonquin, 1984.

Moody, Samuel B. *Reprieve from Hell*. Orlando, Fla.: Samuel B. Moody and Maury Allen, Mfg., 1961.

Nix, Asbury L. *Corregidor—Oasis of Hope*. Amherst, WI: Palmer, 1991.

Peart, Cecil J. *Peart's Journal*. Navy Medical Archives, 1988.

Rupp, Albert. *Threshold of Hell*. Long Beach, CA: Alman Press, 1983.

Taylor, Vince. *Cabanatuan—Japanese Death Camp*. Waco, TX: Texian, 1987.

Villarin, Mariano. *We Remember Bataan and Corregidor*. Baltimore: Gateway, 1990.

Waldron, Ben. *Corregidor—From Paradise to Hell*. Freeman, SC: Pine Hill Press, 1988.

Wright, John M., Jr. *Captured on Corregidor—Diary of an American POW in World War II*. Jefferson, NC: McFarland, 1988.

INDEX